Celine DION

Tour de Force

GEORGES-HÉBERT GERMAIN

PUBLICATIONS INTERNATIONAL, LTD.

Canadian Georges-Hébert Germain is a well-known reporter, interviewer, and author. He has had a dozen books appear on the best-seller list in his home province of Quebec, and has won many journalism awards, including two President's Medals for Excellence. Céline and her husband René asked Georges-Hébert to write an honest account of their lives. That book, *Celine,* was a best-seller in Quebec and France. Currently Georges-Hébert is working on an IMAX film to be released in the fall of 1999.

Photo credits

Front cover: **Michael Thompson**

Back cover: **John Barrett/Globe Photos, Inc.** (right); **Neal Preston/Outline** (left).

AP/Wide World Photos: Frank Micelotta: 63; Massimo Sambucetti: 119 (bottom); Kathy Willens: 77; **Archive Photos/ Reuters:** Gary Hershorn: 111; Fred Prouser: 119 (top); **George Bodnar:** 50, 70, 72, 73, 80, 81, 101; **CBS, Inc.:** 126; **Canapress:** 66, 106; **Celebrity Photo:** Scott Downie: 30; Gilbert Flores: Table of contents (bottom), 125 (top); Miranda Shen: 125 (bottom); **Corbis:** Anita Bugge/SIN: 83, 87, 105; M. Gerber: 57, 99; Pacha: 54; **Globe Photos, Inc.:** Mark Allan/Alpha: 79; John Barrett: 55, 65, 69, 75, 76, 91, 109; Dave Parker/Alpha: 118 (top); Andrea Renault: 100; **Harpo, Inc.:** 39; **London Features International:** David Hum: 34 (bottom), 110, 113; Ilpo Musto: 117; Ron Wolfson: 23, 123; **MVM/Budde Music France:** 126; **Martin Photography:** 28; **Official White House Photo:** 36; **Outline:** Neal Preston: 7, 49, 84, 95; Retna Ltd.: Arnal/Geral/Stills: 51; E. Catarina: 103; E. Catarina/Stills: 85; George Bodnar: 114, 124; R. Corlouer: 89, 97; Bill Davila: 96; Gary Gershoff: 47, 61; Sandra Johnson: 48; Gerard Schachmes/Regards: Table of contents (center), 53, 122 (bottom); Justin Thomas/All Action: 121; **Christoph Ruckstuhl/Keystone:** 122 (top); **Dimo Safari:** 31, 67, 107; **Sony Music Entertainment, Inc./550 Music/Epic Records Group:** 45, 126; **Sony Music Entertainment, Inc./Epic Records Group:** 126; **Sony Music Entertainment, Inc./Columbia:** 126; **Sygma:** Stephane Cardinale: 92; Pierre-Paul Poulin: 58; **TC/Groupe Quebecor, Inc.:** 126.

Additional photography courtesy of Feeling Productions Inc.

Contents

Foreword

TODAY, MUCH IS MADE IN THE MEDIA ABOUT THOSE WHO ARE IN THE PUBLIC EYE. SOME OF THE STORIES ARE TRUE. MANY ARE NOT. AS YOU READ THE PAGES OF THIS BOOK YOU WILL FIND A FAITHFUL PORTRAIT OF A VERY EXCITING TIME IN MY LIFE, MY "FALLING INTO YOU" TOUR. YOU WILL ALSO READ ABOUT HOW I GREW UP HAPPILY IN A FAMILY OF 14 CHILDREN, ALWAYS KNOWING THAT I WANTED TO SING.

RENÉ AND I ESPECIALLY WANTED TO BE ABLE TO RECOGNIZE OURSELVES AND THE PEOPLE AROUND US IN THE PAGES OF THE BOOK. TO GET TO KNOW US BETTER, GEORGES-HÉBERT GERMAIN SHARED OUR LIVES FOR MORE THAN A YEAR. HE SAW US LAUGH. HE SAW US CRY AND FIGHT AND KISS AND TELL EACH OTHER, "I LOVE YOU." HE LIVED AS PART OF THE FAMILY THAT HAS FORMED AROUND US, A FAMILY MADE UP OF FRIENDS, ASSOCIATES, FELLOW ARTISTS . . . AND OF FANS.

SO PLEASE READ ABOUT MY ROMANCE WITH MY HUSBAND—AND MY ROMANCE WITH MY AUDIENCE. MY LOVE OF SINGING AND MY LOVE OF THE SIMPLE THINGS IN LIFE. MY LOVE/HATE RELATIONSHIP WITH THE STAGE. AND MY DEEP AFFECTION FOR THE "FAMILY" THAT TRAVELS WITH ME ON TOUR. YOU WILL SEE YOURSELF IN THE STORY TOO, AS YOU ARE WHEN I SING ON STAGE IN FRONT OF YOU. I HOPE YOU ENJOY THIS PORTRAIT OF US.

ONCE AGAIN, I HAVE WHAT I WISHED FOR. GEORGES-HÉBERT HAS WRITTEN AN HONEST AND INTIMATE STORY FOR MY FANS—A CANDID STORY OF MY LIFE, ON AND OFF STAGE.

YOU KNOW I SING FOR YOU, AND THAT YOU ARE PART OF MY FAMILY.

Céline

Céline

A FAMILY AFFAIR

ADHÉMAR AND THÉRÈSE DION'S FAMILY WAS FILLED OUT IN 1968 WITH THE BIRTH OF THEIR FOURTEENTH CHILD, CÉLINE. THE DIONS ALL REMEMBER THE DAY OF CÉLINE'S BIRTH. IT WAS UNDER THE SIGN OF THE RAM, SATURDAY, MARCH 30, 1968, THE YEAR OF THE MONKEY, IN THE AFTERNOON. BABY CÉLINE WAS TO SPEND THE FIRST TWO YEARS OF HER LIFE IN THE ARMS OF HER MOTHER, HER FATHER, OR ONE OF HER 13 BROTHERS AND SISTERS. CÉLINE WAS THE CENTER OF INTEREST FOR 15 OTHER PEOPLE. HER "PUBLIC" LOVED AND ADORED HER.

PEOPLE FORGET OVER TIME. EVERYONE DOES. BUT CÉLINE'S MEMORIES ARE HELPED ALONG BY STORIES THAT HER BROTHERS AND SISTERS TELL HER. AND HER MOTHER LOVES TO RELATE THE LITTLE DETAILS OF HER CHILDHOOD. THERE'S HER BROTHER MICHEL'S WEDDING WHEN, AT AGE FIVE, CÉLINE FIRST SANG IN PUBLIC. OR THAT TERRIBLE TIME WHEN THEY LEARNED THAT KARINE, HER SISTER LIETTE'S DAUGHTER, HAD BEEN DIAGNOSED WITH CYSTIC FIBROSIS. OR THE ACCIDENT THAT ALMOST TOOK CÉLINE'S LIFE IN THE SPRING OF 1970. CÉLINE KNOWS ALL THE STORIES BY HEART.

THE DIONS

CÉLINE USED TO SING ALL THE TIME FOR HER MOTHER AND FATHER AND HER SIBLINGS. IN THE EVENING AFTER SUPPER, THEY URGED HER TO CLIMB ONTO THE KITCHEN TABLE AND PRESSED AN IMAGINARY MICROPHONE INTO HER HAND—USUALLY A SPOON OR A PENCIL. SHE WOULD SING FOR AN ENTIRE HOUR. BUT SHE NEVER DARED PERFORM OUTSIDE THE HOUSE UNTIL HER BROTHER MICHEL'S WEDDING, ON AUGUST 18, 1973. SHE SANG A FOLK TUNE, SHE WORE A HAT AND GLOVES AND A TULLE DRESS. THE NIGHT BEFORE, SHE'D REHEARSED WITH HER MOTHER. WHEN THE TIME CAME, SHE STEPPED UP NEXT TO THE PIANO (PLAYED BY HER BROTHER DANIEL). A SMILE WAS FROZEN ON HER FACE AND HER EYES WERE FOCUSED ON THE GROUND. BUT AS SOON AS SHE STARTED SINGING, HER STAGE FRIGHT DISAPPEARED. SHE FELT AS THOUGH SHE WAS BEING CARRIED FAR AWAY BY A

Opposite page: *At age 16, Céline had exceptional talent; she knew how to use it, and she was gifted with steely determination. There was no stopping her. This was the year she sang "Une colombe" ("A Dove") before Pope John Paul II. After that appearance, the song became a smash hit all across Quebec, and Céline Dion's career took a giant step forward.*

Céline's childhood was filled with warmth and love. From the start, she was the center of interest for 15 other people—her parents, Adhémar and Thérèse Dion, and her 13 siblings. She grew up in Charlemagne, a country town just east of Montreal, in French-speaking Quebec.

magic breath of wind. For the first time in her life, Céline felt how good it can be to be watched and listened to.

Two weeks later, on the first Tuesday of September, 1973, Céline Dion began kindergarten. She was miserable. She'd always been with adults and older children; what fun was it to get to know kindergartners? It was even worse the next year when she started first grade—her mother took a job. That meant that every day Céline ate lunch at her sister Louise's house on Pierre Street, and she slept there on Thursday and Friday nights when her mother had to work. In the evening, alone in her bed, Céline would weep.

Céline was nine when they were told that two-month-old Karine had cystic fibrosis. It happened on a Sunday. Karine was sent to the Sainte-Justine hospital by ambulance. There, Liette, the Dion's fourth child, was told that her daughter should be baptized immediately.

Céline heard her parents say that Karine would never have the chance to grow up. Perhaps because of that, Céline was deeply affected by what was happening to Karine. She was the first child Céline felt close to; Céline, who was only happy in the company of adults, loved Karine. For Céline, Karine was her reminder that the world is a hard and unforgiving place.

○   ○   ○   ○   ○

That summer, Céline's father Adhémar, with his daughter Claudette, bought a restaurant-bar called Vieux

Baril—the old barrel—where for years the Dion children sang. Paul, who was 15 by then, decided to buy an electric organ and started playing there. The Vieux Baril quickly became a popular meeting place.

Céline saw her first real shows at the Vieux Baril. She faced her first crowds there, and had her first successes out of the family circle on its stage. Sometimes they found her at 4:00 A.M., asleep in a booth. Her mother told her, "You can stay up as late as you want, as long as you can wake up the next morning for school." And the next morning, remembering her promise, and not wanting to miss out on the pleasures of late-night music, she dragged herself off to school, no matter how tired she was.

Céline already knew what she wanted to do with her life. She waited, she dreamed, she imagined herself on the stage, in the recording studio, facing the crowds. Her mother frequently found her standing in front of the television, imitating female vocalists. At the Vieux Baril, people were so amazed by her repertoire that they paid her for special requests; her parents were amazed at how she now faced the public without fear.

When the Vieux Baril burned down, it was a personal disaster for Céline. She had gotten used to the crowds, the applause, the laughter and cheering, and now she couldn't do without it. Her mother understood completely. Thérèse Tanguay-Dion always had a very clear idea of what show business was. When she felt her daughter was ready she would approach Réne Angélil, the man who represented Quebecois music star Ginette Reno. For Mrs. Dion, that fact alone made him the most important producer and the best manager anywhere.

IT WAS ONLY A DREAM

In the spring of 1981, Michel called Angélil to remind him of a cassette tape that had arrived in his office—in a brown envelope with a red rubber band around it. He told him that he'd be wrong not to open it. Dion added that he was sure Angélil hadn't listened to it yet. If he had, he would have responded by now. Angélil knew Michel from the days when Michel was the singer for a group called The Show. Angélil also knew that the Dions were a musical family, and he respected Michel's opinion when it came to popular music. René promised Michel that he'd listen to the tape.

Angélil called Michel Dion ten minutes later and asked if his sister could come and see him. "When?" Michel asked.

"Now."

Céline (center row, third from the right) with her classmates at St. Jude School. School never held much appeal for her. She already knew what she wanted to do with her life. As she daydreamed in class, she imagined herself on-stage, in the recording studio, facing the crowds.

Around 2:00 that afternoon, "the Dion girl" showed up—with her mother. Céline was a tiny little thing, painfully shy, badly dressed, not very pretty, with buck teeth, a pointy chin, and very thick eyebrows. But her eyes were extraordinary. They took in everything, big brown eyes brimming over with intelligence. Angélil spoke to her gently.

Hoping to please him, Céline told him that her favorite singer—her idol—was Ginette Reno, whom Angélil represented, and that she knew all Reno's songs by heart. She said she'd even seen her once at the Place-des-Arts in Montreal. So, René asked her to sing as though *she* were on stage at the Place-des-Arts.

Céline told him she was used to singing with a microphone, or something she could hold as one. Angélil handed her a pencil. Céline stood up, took a few steps back, and began to sing. In a matter of seconds it was as though she were standing on the stage of a world-class hall. Her eyes were focused on the upper balconies above Angélil's head. He sat there at his desk; he couldn't believe his eyes or his ears. That little girl had everything: the instincts, a powerful voice, a presence.

Angélil started to cry. Admittedly he was already depressed, but also because the voice he heard was incredibly touching. He was so impressed that when the girl stopped singing, he couldn't even remember her name.

The soft-spoken Angélil told Mrs. Dion, "If you trust me, I guarantee you that in five years, your daughter will be a big star in Quebec and France."

Mrs. Dion wasn't surprised by Mr. Angélil's enthusiasm. It was as if she'd expected it.

THE VOICE OF HEAVEN

By the spring of 1981, René Angélil was friends with the family. He showered Mrs. Dion with flowers and gifts, buying Céline all kinds of records, sweaters, dresses, a Walkman, taking her to restaurants with her parents and brothers and sisters. According to Angélil, he had a plan and ideas, the means and the time to push Céline's career ahead.

He wanted Michel Jasmin to be the first to present Céline to the Quebec public. At the time, Jasmin hosted the biggest talk show on television in Quebec. In mid-June, René played Céline's demo "Ce n'était qu'un rêve" ("It Was Only a Dream") for Jasmin, who immediately promised to put Céline on the show. René called Céline to give her the good news. His call turned the Dion household upside down. That very day, Mrs. Dion began making a pink dress for her daughter—"pink's your favorite color, it suits you so well, child"—gathered at the waist with bouffant sleeves. Three long nights' work. She located some pink stockings to go with it. But no pink shoes could be found. Mrs. Dion bought red ones and dyed them.

Céline went on Jasmin's show on June 19, 1981, a Friday, just as her 45

Céline has always loved her fans. Signing autographs and being in touch with the people has always been important to her, even from the very beginning.

"Ce n'était qu'un rêve" hit the stores. Angélil arrived at the studio very early with Céline and her mother. He introduced them to everyone—from Jasmin to the hair stylist.

Céline was horribly nervous. During rehearsals, she couldn't look at the wide, cold eye of the camera. "You've got to dive right in," René told her. "Look at the camera. Act like your mother's watching you through it, she's on the other side of it. She's listening to you, and she loves you."

Céline felt like he was asking her to jump off a cliff. She was afraid of forgetting the words to the song, and she was afraid her voice would break. For good luck, she wanted to knock on wood, but there wasn't any in the studio. She spotted a briar pipe in an ashtray, and she touched that.

As soon as she started taping, her nervousness disappeared. She looked straight into the camera, knowing that through it, at least one million people were watching and listening to her. For a fleeting, marvelous moment she was completely happy. Several times she let her eyes come to rest on the studio audience. In the dark hall, she saw her mother and father and her brothers and sisters, who were watching her. She felt as if they were singing along with her.

She finished with a broad smile, and the floor manager gave the audience the "applause" signal. But on her way to the armchair where Michel Jasmin waited, her stage fright returned. She knew how to sing. But when it came to answering questions from a professional interviewer—that was another story.

After the taping, the entire Dion family piled into their living room to watch the show. Céline was still nervous. She hated looking at herself. She didn't like her face: Her teeth stuck out, her eyebrows were too thick, her nose was too big . . . and she hated her accent and the sound of her voice when she answered Michel Jasmin's questions.

But when she sang, her voice was strong and true. She was used to hearing herself that way. She'd spent hours singing, recording herself, then listening to the tapes. She didn't like her nasal tone, and she'd tried to correct it. She'd succeeded, at least some of the time, but there were still echoes of that tone in the higher notes.

On that same show, fate had assembled a wide variety of guests. There was Fernand Gignac (the owner of the briar pipe), singer Bruce Huard, who had starred for the defunct group the Sultans and had given it up when he discovered God, and Rodger Brulotte, public relations director for the Montreal Expos baseball team. After Céline had sung, Brulotte told Angélil how wonderful she

was. Thinking fast, Angélil asked him whether Céline could sing the national anthem at an Expos game.

During the summer of 1981, Céline Dion did the honors several times at Montreal's Olympic Stadium. She even had a special Expos uniform made for her. Just before the game, the announcer told the crowd that the U.S. and Canadian national anthems would be sung by "a 13-year-old girl, Céline Dion." Microphone in hand, she ran onto the field and up to the mound. Facing the crowd, the players, and the TV cameras, she belted out "O Canada" and "The Star-Spangled Banner." She had no idea what the words of the second song meant, since she'd only memorized them. But she wasn't afraid. The crowd and the cameras didn't scare her. The anthems moved her. She took off on their wings.

On October 31, 1981, she was featured on page one of the entertainment

In 1981, Céline's first two albums were released only a few weeks apart. The first was The Voice of Heaven (La Voix du Bon Dieu)*, and the second was a Christmas album. Over that winter, the 13-year-old would sell tens of thousands of the albums.*

section in the daily paper *La Presse.* "Céline Dion, at thirteen: Will she be the next Judy Garland?" the headline asked. For the first time, the whole story was told by a journalist named Denis Lavoie: her musical family, her 13 brothers and sisters, a father who built his own house outside Montreal, a mother who wrote songs and sewed dresses, her meeting with René Angélil and with French songwriter Eddy Marnay, her talent, intelligence, and determination.

Réne made it possible for Céline to record two albums that fall. The album jacket of the first release presented two sides of Céline's personality. On the back, a well-behaved, gentle child whose eyes are averted, as if she were listening carefully to someone. There is sparkle in those big dark eyes, and a pout on her lips. Her cheeks are round like a child's. Her hair falls freely onto her pink sweater. But on the front of the jacket, there's a made-up young woman. In her long fingers with pink, polished nails, she's holding a flowery parasol that rests on her shoulder. She gazes down at us, right in the eyes, with a conquering look. The record cover shows the girl-child attentively listening to someone, and the young woman who has mastered her image as well as she's mastered her voice.

Three weeks later, in early December, René Angélil launched *Céline Dion Sings Christmas.* During the winter of 1981–82, several tens of thousands of the two albums were sold. On March 30,

1982, the day Céline turned 14, Angélil founded TBS Productions, their first business venture.

Fortunately, Céline was all but over her shyness. She discovered she liked talking. She was open, honest, and free in her conversation. And charming too. She wasn't the prettiest girl, but everyone who met her remembered her lively spirit, her intelligence, her spontaneity—and her eyes.

BOUND FOR GLORY

Céline was listening to a lot of American music. Often, all alone in front of the mirror in the upstairs room, a hairbrush or a pen in her hand instead of a microphone, she would sing Aretha Franklin or Stevie Wonder songs, faithfully reproducing their intonations. She was singing with her soul, without worrying about what the words meant.

She'd developed a regular obsession for *Flashdance.* She'd seen the movie so often she knew it by heart, scene by

Céline used to use anything as a "microphone" when she was a child—a fork, a crayon, a pencil. She always knew she wanted to sing, and every member of her family encouraged her dream.

scene. The film tells the story of a poor girl, a welder by trade, very much on her own, though beautiful. Her dream is to dance! She studies by herself, seeking her way. One day she meets an older lady who once was the prima ballerina in a classical ballet company. She tells the younger woman that she has talent enough, and that she needs to find the balance, harmony, beauty, and strength inside herself to succeed. She must learn without the benefit of schools; she must not accept other people's vision of her. The older woman tells her, "If you give up your dream, you die."

Céline loved that story about raw talent and wild ambition and the need for absolute freedom. Best of all, there was the music. One song in particular struck her. She practiced it hundreds of times in front of the mirror, then she sang it a capella for her brothers and sisters. The song was "What a Feeling," and she swore that one day she'd sing it onstage.

BEGINNINGS

Céline's life was a hundred times more exciting than most kids her age. In April 1982, Liette, Karine's mother, met Denis Mouton in a hospital waiting room. Mr. Mouton was the president of the Quebec Association for Cystic Fibrosis, and he was looking for someone to head up the spring fund-raising campaign. He stopped looking when he discovered that Liette was the sister of Céline Dion. Céline had sung on dozens of stages across Quebec and had been inter-

viewed by many journalists. Her songs were playing on the radio every day. She was making more money in one month than her father did in a whole year. In Quebec, she was already a star on the way up. Céline co-sponsored the campaign along with Quebec singer Gilles Vigneault.

On July 1, 1982, Céline's brothers and sisters and a few wives and husbands went to Mirabel Airport to wish Céline "bon voyage." Her mother and René were also on the plane. While the other girls and boys in her class spent the summer in Charlemagne or the surrounding countryside, riding their bikes, watching TV, or even working part-time in fast-food outlets, she was going to Paris. To cut an album with professional artists.

○   ○   ○   ○   ○

One September evening, her songwriter, Eddy Marnay, called from Paris to say that the song "Tellement j'ai d'amour pour toi" had been selected to represent France in a big international contest the next month in Japan. Eddy's news was so fabulous and unexpected that she didn't know what to say. "Yes, all right . . . I don't really know . . . I'll have to ask Mom," she stammered. Mrs. Dion spoke to Eddy, and Céline heard her say that her daughter could go to Japan to sing in the contest, and she would go with her.

No sooner had she hung up than the phone rang again. It was René Angélil. He had all the details: the figures, the

At 14, Céline started winning awards for her music. Here she is with her parents, Adhémar and Thérèse—her two greatest fans—and two of her awards.

dates, the names. It was the 13th Yamaha World Popular Song Festival in Tokyo. Out of 1,907 songs submitted by 49 countries, 30 songs had been selected. Céline set out for Japan with her mother, René, and René's good friend, Ben Kaye.

LAND OF THE RISING SUN

The first round of the Yamaha Festival took place on Friday and Saturday, October 29 and 30, 1982. Céline was to appear on Friday. Each contestant chose a number at random to determine when they'd sing. Céline ended up with five, which was pronounced "go" in Japanese. She performed well, received warm applause from the audience and good marks from the judges. She was one of ten performers selected for the grand finale that would take place on Sunday afternoon in Tokyo's Budokan Hall, a large amphitheater that could seat 12,000 people. For the final perfor-

mance, she also drew number five—"go." But because she was so close to her goal, she felt tense and nervous.

She stood while she waited her turn so her homemade white cotton dress wouldn't get wrinkled. She noticed a coin lying at the foot of the stairway to the stage. She picked it up. It had the number five on it, so she kept it, just for luck. But her dress had no pockets, so she slipped it into her shoe just before she went up the steps. And as she moved toward the spotlights to sing "Tellement j'ai d'amour pour toi," she could feel the coin, her good luck charm, under the arch of her right foot.

It was the first time she'd sung before such a large audience. Besides the 12,000 people who filled the Budokan, there were millions of viewers watching the festival on TV.

In the end, Céline shared the grand prize with Mexican singer Yoshio, but she garnered another distinction as well. Impressed by her talent and charisma, the 62 musicians gave her the Orchestra's Special Award.

With the Tokyo victory, Céline Dion turned into a major star in Quebec practically overnight. The next morning she was front-page news, talked about on radio and TV. People were intrigued. Céline had sold more than 100,000 copies of her first album, but she was relatively unknown outside of show business and the recording industry. Who was this 14-year-old girl from Quebec, and why had she represented France in a major international competition? The tabloids set off in search of the answers. Where did she come from? How old was she really? What color were her eyes? What did she like to do? Who was her boyfriend?

When she returned, a crowd greeted her at the airport. There were loads of flowers, stuffed frogs and teddy bears, cameras and microphones. René Lévesque, the premier of the province of Quebec, insisted on meeting her personally and congratulating her in the name of all citizens. A few days later, at the Montreal Forum, some 10,000 people gave her a deafening ovation when she came onstage. The next day, she was back on page one. Not only had she won in Tokyo, but she'd charmed the Forum with her openness and the astonishing power of her voice. In only one and a half years, she'd become an important figure in Quebec show business.

BROADENING HER APPEAL

In October 1983, there was to be a celebration for the opening of a new theater in Montreal. Several top artists were invited, including Céline. The theater was to be named after Félix Leclerc, a singer-songwriter from Quebec who was also a writer and poet. René Angélil knew that the intellectuals and cultural types who would patronize that theater thought that Céline was too commercial and too popular for their taste, and they thought her incredible success had come too easily. But Angélil knew that she could broaden her appeal.

Financially, the performance wasn't very rewarding, but artistically it was. Very intensely, very seriously, Céline sang a Félix Leclerc song called "Bozo." It's the story of a poor, simple-minded man who falls desperately in love, and who's caught in a web of impossible dreams. That night, she revealed a new side of her talent. Not only could she sing songs expressly written for her, she could also do justice to the more difficult classics.

At the 1983 Quebec Music Awards (the Félix Awards) ceremonies, Céline won four awards: Album of the Year, Female Singer of the Year, Most Popular Artist on the International Scene, and Revelation of the Year. She wept openly—tears of joy—every time she went on stage to receive her trophies.

In show business, one success leads to another. Not only are prizes a good indicator of popularity, they also stimulate sales. The four Félix Awards boosted her fortunes. The money started rolling in. It rolled out just as fast. "If you want your rocket to take off," Angélil liked to say, "you have to use the very best fuel."

"A DOVE"

They were in Paris in early summer 1984 to cut the demos for a new album when Angélil got a call from a woman named Sylvie Lalande. She and Angélil met for lunch in a little Lebanese restaurant to talk about a citywide centennial celebration that was being planned for a Montreal newspaper. She mentioned that Pope John Paul II would be visiting Montreal that September in time for the celebrations.

The Church wanted to use the event to stress the importance of young people and their concerns, visions, and expectations of today's world. For several weeks the organizers worked on the central themes of the celebration and its stage show: love, suicide, divorce, racism, violence, world hunger. The budget was enormous, and an army of volunteers was ready to get to work. The stage would hold 2,000 people. Religious songs would be sung. Under choreographer Hugo de Po's direction, actors carrying white banners would create the figure of an enormous dove spreading her wings.

Composer Paul Baillargeon and songwriter Marcel Lefebvre decided to write a song to bring the whole theme together. Naturally, their song was entitled "A Dove." They went looking for a young voice to sing it, and they chose Céline Dion. She was young and she was a top-selling artist. Who could fail to be thrilled by her voice?

That same evening, Sylvie met Céline and her parents at their hotel. Angélil made everyone laugh when he described how Mrs. Dion reacted. She simply couldn't believe that her daughter would sing for the Pope. She was sure someone was playing a practical joke on her.

On September 11, dressed all in white, her long hair cascading down her back, in front of the Pope and 60,000 people waving white handkerchiefs, Céline Dion sang "Une colombe" ("A Dove"). The day had been windy and rainy. An hour before the ceremonies were to begin, people were expecting the worst. But when Michel Jasmin, who was doing the introductions, stepped onstage, the sky suddenly changed. Strong winds chased away the remaining clouds. Sun filled the stadium.

Céline cried as she sang the song. But her tears didn't alter her voice. It re-

Céline's career was gaining momentum. In 1983, she walked away from the Quebec Music Awards with four Félix Awards. She shed tears of joy every time she walked onto the stage.

Céline meets with Pope John Paul II in Rome in 1985.

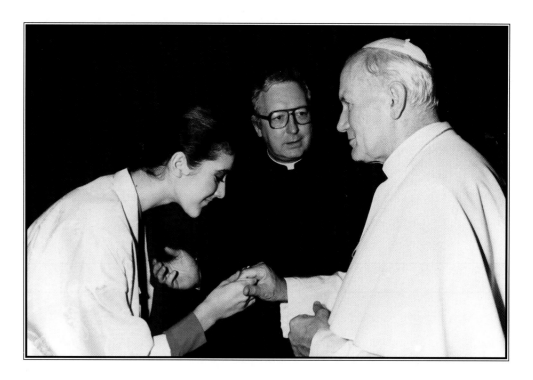

mained strong and firm. By the next day, her song had become a smash hit all across Quebec.

On October 15, 1984, Céline accepted two more Félix Awards (Top-Selling Album and Female Singer of the Year) in a teary ceremony. Then she jetted off to Paris to promote her *Mélanie* album. In 1981, René Angélil had promised Mrs. Dion that in five years Céline would be a big star in Quebec and France. He kept his promise—in less than three years.

During their long European sojourn, they traveled to Rome to meet the Pope, who granted them a private audience. René was very impressed, and asked His Holiness to bless his family and Céline's.

❍   ❍   ❍   ❍   ❍

Céline celebrated her seventeenth birthday on the stage of Le Carrefour College, in northern Quebec. In a little

over two months, she gave 36 performances in 25 cities in Quebec, Ontario, and New Brunswick. The show grew as she traveled. Her name was on everyone's lips. She traveled in a minibus, while the equipment followed along in a truck. As they rolled into Tracadie in the province of New Brunswick, they saw giant banners reading, "Welcome, Céline." Wherever she went, she played to sold-out halls.

❍   ❍   ❍   ❍   ❍

That spring, René and Céline founded their own company, called Feeling Productions Inc. According to Angélil, to reach the widest possible audience, you had to start slowly. And Céline believed him. She drank in his words. In her eyes, he was wisdom, experience, intelligence, strength, and security, all rolled into one. He took care of everything. He made sure she had whatever she wanted. When she and her mother were on tour, they ate in the best restaurants and slept in the best hotels.

Mrs. Dion loved being on tour. She liked seeing the countryside, comparing the cities and towns and people. But Adhémar Dion was 62 years old. Join the tour? No thanks. "I've knocked around enough in this life of mine." When Céline sang in Montreal, he would go and see her, cheering at the top of his lungs. When the show ended, he'd leap to his feet and shout out his admiration. People around him stared. "That's my daughter," he'd explain. That was good enough for him. He was her greatest fan, and that's all he wanted to be.

Mrs. Dion had plenty to do on the tour. She helped her daughter choose her wardrobe, her makeup, and her hairstyle. She was an excellent critic too. Every night, she watched the show from somewhere in the hall and wrote down her comments. Sometimes she would criticize one of Céline's movements, or a problem with her dress, or a missed cue, or a wrong expression in the song presentations.

○   ○   ○   ○   ○

In the 1985 edition of the Félix Awards, Céline was a bigger winner than ever. She won for Best-Selling Song, Best-Selling Album, Best Female Singer, Best Pop Song, and Best Pop Album. As usual, the happy winner shed tears of joy. But there was something else. She was about to enter a time that filled her with fear. René had decided to put things on hold for a year at the end of this tour. In the coming year, she would be going into some dark pathways. But right now, she was in the spotlight, her Best Female Singer Award in her hand, while her fans looked on. She thanked René Angélil…and burst into tears again.

René had been in a popular band in the '60s and knew what it was like to hear the applause, and he wondered how Céline would get along without that thrill during the year-long break they'd agreed to take. A singer would need both steely determination and strength of character to disappear at the height of her popularity. It wasn't that big a risk; Céline had shown she was here to stay. Not only could she sing and make records, she could perform onstage and on TV, and she knew how to talk to crowds and journalists. She was going to get prettier, she was going to grow up— then she'd come back with a vengeance.

Soon Céline would take leave of her public, and that wouldn't be easy. Her audiences had been the only thing that could fill the emptiness that came from not being able to love the only man she really wanted. An older man who she thought didn't love her, and who seemed as unhappy as he could be.

METAMORPHOSIS

Céline found plenty to do while René was away. She was in the mood for a change. She wanted to be someone else, physically. An orthodontist was called in. She'd have to wear braces for several months. She learned English and went

As Céline's confidence grew, so, too, did her ability to make changes in her appearance. Getting her hair cut was a big step—but one that she loved immediately. Her sensuality was becoming more apparent, as was the fact that she was in love.

He had promised to cut an English record with her. "Singing in English isn't good enough," he told Céline, "you have to speak it too." So Céline went to Berlitz to learn English. Nine hours a day, five days a week, for six months. Musicians and singers usually have a good ear for languages—since language is music. But sometimes, the beginnings can be rough. Céline felt as though she were drowning. She couldn't understand any human language, she stuttered and stammered, her ideas got mixed up. Then little by little, very slowly, everything became clear, and she found herself speaking English.

She spent a lot of time at the movies and listened to the widest possible variety of music. She got a new hairstyle and a new look—the playful teenager was about to turn into a sensuous woman. The first thing to go were her floppy pants and her turtleneck sweaters.

In Céline's life and career, big changes were about to take place. Céline had completed her metamorphosis from moth to butterfly. She and Angélil were ready for new adventures. They wanted to change everything: the look, the sound, the material, the music.

back to work with choreographer Peter George. She'd make herself into a seductive young woman, and the man she loved would have to notice her.

Céline Dion was 17 years old and madly in love with René. Judging from the songs he wrote for the new album, *C'est pour toi* (*It's for You*), Eddy Marnay must have intuitively known her feelings for her manager. Through the songs, Céline spoke to the man she desired, but who didn't see her in the same light.

But René Angélil was either blind or pretending to be blind.

When I think back at everything that's happened, at my life, I have to admit that I've been a very lucky girl. It's incredible. The further René and I went, the better things got, the more doors opened for us. I guess I was born under a lucky star.

The 1987 Juno Awards ceremony (the Canadian version of the Grammys) was to be held in November, and Angélil accepted the Juno invitation—as long as Céline could sing in English. They set off for Toronto, all terribly nervous. Everyone would be there. It would be a who's who of Canadian show business.

Once she was onstage with the audience and the cameras, all nervousness disappeared. She performed the first composition written for her in English, "Have a Heart," with pleasure and passion and mastery. In return, she received thunderous applause. René wept openly. He realized that Céline had just opened another door. The next day, the record company scouts and decision-makers would be chasing after him. One critic wrote, "She blew everybody away." Céline Dion had stolen the show at the Juno gala.

René invited Carol Reynolds, head of variety programs at the Canadian Broadcasting Corporation (CBC), to catch Céline's show at the Théâtre Saint-Denis, in the heart of Montreal's Latin Quarter. She accepted the invitation immediately, and she was bowled over. Not only by the performance, but by the fans' response. After the show Céline, René, and Carol met in a restaurant across the street from the theater. Céline, whose English was improving rapidly, talked to her about her dream album. The one she wanted to record with David Foster. But Foster wasn't returning their calls. He was too busy with

Neil Diamond, Barbra Streisand, Paul McCartney, and all the other stars who used his services as arranger and producer.

As luck would have it, Carol Reynolds was leaving in a few days for Los Angeles, Foster's hometown. She just happened to know him—and she promised to show him the Juno Awards video.

One afternoon less than a week later, Angélil got a call from Carol Reynolds. "I've got someone on the line who'd like to talk to you." It was David Foster. Carol had shown him the Juno video and played her song, "Incognito." He found Céline "outstanding," and was convinced she had what it took to break into the U.S. market. She could sing like no one else, and she had "that little something extra" that people were looking for. The support of a top international producer like Foster was the opportunity of a lifetime.

Working with top international producer David Foster was a longtime goal for Céline and René. Foster (at the piano) became a huge force in her career, as well as a good friend in their personal lives.

FIRST STIRRINGS

In 1988, Céline represented Switzerland in the Eurovision Awards. This year they were held in Dublin, and Céline had been tapped as the odds-on favorite to win. And she did. As he did after every performance, René joined Céline in her room and told her his version of the evening. He told her everything he saw, heard, and felt. She sat there at the head of the bed, her legs crossed under the blankets, happy to be alone with the man she loved. She could listen to him talk all night and the next day and for all time to come. Her mother, her brothers, and her sisters—they all knew she was wildly in love with him, and they had known it for a long time. But did he know?

His story ended. René sat at the foot of the bed, saying not a word. Céline looked at him. Then he got slowly to his feet, wished her good night, and walked toward the door.

Every night, ever since their first tour together in the winter of 1985, when they stayed in hotels and motels in small Quebec towns, the routine was the same. He gave her a little kiss on the cheek and wished her good night. Nothing changed when they went to Paris for a recording session, or to Toronto for the Juno Awards ceremony.

And now, on this night of triumph and victory, he was about to leave without even a kiss. The door was already open. He smiled. She came up to him, pressed herself tight against him. "You didn't kiss me, René Angélil." Her head and eyes were turned downward.

He didn't realize what had happened, even though he'd thought of that very scene a thousand times over the last few weeks, imagined it a hundred times. He bent toward her and kissed her on the lips, the neck, and wrapped his arms around her in a powerful embrace. Then he dropped his arms and rushed off to his room. For an instant she stood there, speechless.

Then she called out to him, "If you don't come back, I'll knock on your door."

THE GOSSIP LINE

While the most powerful professionals of the recording world were fine-tuning and packaging her songs in their Montreal, New York, London, Los Angeles, and Toronto offices, and while they were hard at work on promotion plans for her first album in English, Céline Dion was spending a few days with her parents in the big white house in Sainte-Anne-des-Lacs. It was fall, and the weather was fine and warm. Céline was perfectly happy. Almost.

She was 21. She had an accountant, a notary, an agent, and millions of fans. As a spokeswoman for Chrysler, she was happily driving that year's Laser Turbo. She owned two houses. She was famous in Quebec and France. The toughest honchos, the top pros of American show business, were fascinated by her voice and talent. She was rich. She traveled. She loved shopping in the world's priciest shops. She owned more than 200 pairs of shoes, more than 100 dresses, three fur coats, drawerfuls of the finest lingerie—whatever she wanted. Almost.

For the last three days, she'd been raking and gathering up the fallen leaves from around her house. She packed them into orange garbage bags and lined them up along the driveway. She was humming to herself, inventing a tune, a melodic line she would toy with for hours on end, softening it, breaking it down, starting over again.

Journalists want to know everything, right down to the most intimate thoughts and desires of the stars. And if you try to hide things from them, they'll just invent a story—sometimes even the truth that you were trying to conceal. It's always better to come clean.

But Céline couldn't open her heart. And the lie she was forced to tell cast a shadow over her happiness, a shadow that darkened and confused her. René didn't want people talking about their love affair. He was afraid people would be scandalized. After all, he was more than twice her age, twice divorced, with three children.

She'd just completed her very first album in English. All of the 12 songs were about love—about burning, over-powering passion. She was going to fly off to Nassau to tape a video clip that would show her as a sexy young lady with plenty of experience in the ways of love. The press photos for the launch of her *Unison* album showed her as entic-

ing, with tight jeans and a form-fitting top that bared her shoulders and sun-tanned tummy.

It was all a game, of course. All in the name of showbiz. In real life she had to pretend she was a girl with no inter-est in love. On the screen and in her songs she was all woman and then some. The world of show business is all ap-pearance and illusion, where anything goes. But her songs, videos, and photos let Céline tell the truth. She wanted to be as frank and honest as she could in real life. She wanted the whole world to know that she loved René Angélil, and that he loved her.

She was just about finished raking up the dead leaves that covered the lawn, just like the perfectionist she is. She likes to have things in order. Straightening up the place where she lives is a way of putting her emotions, her feelings, her life itself in order. Then her fears evaporate. That's certainly the reason she loves to arrange things, file things away, pile things up, and sort things out in her closets and drawers. Especially when she's in one of her moods. She feels a sense of certainty as everything falls into place, and that gives her a lift and puts her mind at ease.

"One day I'll tell them the name of the man I love. I'll shout it from the rooftops. I'll make him tell the whole world he's nuts about me. He told me so, he tells me every day."

She never lied to her mother. Her mother knew before anyone that her daughter was in love. But it didn't bother her. She was convinced René hadn't noticed, that this kind, handsome man more than 40 years old couldn't possibly be interested in a teenager.

But Céline Dion was no ordinary teenager. By the age of 12 she'd already invested all her intelligence, talent, energy, her entire life in her one great project. At 15 she was a rising star, driven by ambition and a dream. At 18 she was a star in France and Quebec.

Early on, she loved René. For a long time, even she didn't know it. She only knew she was happy. Eddy Marnay spotted the love affair and used it in the songs he wrote for her. Mrs. Dion was convinced her daughter would eventually meet a young man her age and forget all about René. Everybody believed she'd get over it. By then René had realized that Céline was in love. She was entranced by everything he said. Not an hour went by without her inventing some excuse for talking to him on the telephone or seeing him.

In 1986, they hadn't seen much of each other. He had been away in Las Vegas or Nassau much of the time. She was hard at work learning to dance, keeping up with her English lessons, having her teeth straightened. But she thought of him every day.

One day, after they'd been apart for awhile, he came to Duvernay to pick her up to introduce her to some CBS people from Toronto and New York. She answered the door tanned, and wearing a miniskirt and a tank top. Her sister Manon had just done her hair, which tumbled over her bare shoulders. For an instant he just stood there, at a loss for words. She saw how she'd affected him. That day she realized that anything was possible.

In the course of the next year, during the "Incognito" tour, the kiss he planted every night on her cheek edged closer and closer to her lips. Mrs. Dion was far away. They spent more and more time together in long, quiet conversations, in restaurants, in René's car, in Céline's dressing room. Sometimes even when the room was full of people, the two were alone. He talked, she listened and learned. And there were electrifying moments, the triumphs they experienced together that brought them closer to one another and set them apart from the rest.

After they'd admitted their love to each other, René spent hours reminding her, with a thousand and one details, just how it had happened for them. He told her everything—how he admired her, how sexy, beautiful, and brilliant she was. Céline found out that their love had deep, deep roots. It was a story full of twists and turns, of moments, of confessions that they pretended not to see or hear. Twice, a hundred times over they told the same story, just for the pleasure of hearing it again. "The time you came onto the airplane with your navy blue suit," or "the time you came to pick me up in Duvernay," or "the time you fell

Céline and René are never so happy as when they can spend time together. Despite their extremely busy schedules, they always stay in close contact with each other, seeing each other whenever they possibly can. The love they share radiates from them to those who work with them.

asleep on my shoulder," or "the time I pretended to fall asleep on your shoulder." They couldn't get enough.

Angélil had resisted his feelings for the longest time. He was afraid of ruining Céline's life. Of ruining her career. His good friend Eddy Marnay told him, "If you really love her, and I think you do, there's no danger. Love never hurt anyone." Then Marnay added, "Céline is your future. And anyway, you can't hide your love. Not from the people who love you."

A few weeks later, René got a call from Mrs. Dion. From her tone of voice he realized that she knew everything, that she was angry and hurt. "I want to talk to you," she said coldly. She came over to tell him how disappointed she was, that she thought he'd betrayed her. "I trusted you...Céline is my little princess. I wanted a Prince Charming

for her." And instead of a Prince Charming, she'd fallen for a man 26 years older, and twice divorced. She walked out in tears, convinced that he'd destroyed Céline's career and her life.

But Mrs. Dion realized she had no choice. Céline and René lived alone in their own world. They could no longer live without each other. They shared the same soul. Their fates were joined forever.

Everyone in Céline and René's entourage understood. René was worried about how the public would react. But the embargo he'd slapped on their affair would soon be a source of discussion and dissension between the two of them. She would fight back, and she would win. She would take on the man she loved so that their love would win out, so that the whole world would know that they were in love.

There wasn't a single leaf left on the lawn or in the flower beds. Her father could tell her how he liked to let a few lie, they made good fertilizer. She raked up every last one. When she tied up the last bag she felt sad, like the way she felt when a show ended, or when she finished a recording into which she put all her time, her heart, her soul.

THE BATTLE OF QUEBEC

From her room Céline stared at the skiers gliding down floodlit slopes. She was increasingly aware that outside their professional activities, the two of them avoided being seen together. Wherever they went, they booked separate rooms.

At first, she found their little game of hide-and-seek was amusing. One night in Quebec City, she'd even gone out with René wearing a wig and dark glasses. No one recognized her. But after that the urge to tell the whole world about their love had grown stronger. Now it was causing arguments, even fights, between them.

In a few days she'd be 22. Women her age were free to say and do whatever they wanted, to appear in public with the man they loved. Many of them were already married with children. Why should she hide?

René had his reasons. The difference in their ages was the first one. She'd counted the days, including leap years. From January 16, 1942, to March 30, 1968, there are 9,570 days. René had lived all those days without her. But he'd spent so many hours telling her what he'd seen and heard, what he'd done and learned for all those years that she often had the feeling that they belonged to the same generation. He'd given her everything, told her everything. His spirit was in her.

In 1991, for the first time in 20 years, the Juno Awards gala was held in Vancouver, at the Queen Elizabeth Theater. It was raining cats and dogs. A few weeks earlier, "Where Does My Heart Beat Now," the song Céline was to sing that night, vaulted into fourth place on the *Billboard* charts.

Meanwhile, the Canadian "Unison" tour that Céline's booking agent, Barry

When Céline was in Los Angeles in 1990 to sing "Where Does My Heart Beat Now" on the Tonight Show, *she took a stroll down Sunset Boulevard, where posters of her and thousands of copies of* Unison *were on display in the window of Tower Records, the world's most famous record store.*

Garber, put together in January and February was getting under way. Spirits were high. Two Junos, appearances on the *Tonight Show* and *The Late Show,* and a song in fourth place on the *Billboard* charts.

○　○　○　○　○

Fast forward to late spring. The Forum was bursting at the seams. Céline Dion, at 23, was celebrating the first ten years of her career with her fans. The venerable hockey temple's 16,000 seats sold out in a matter of hours. One dollar of every ticket was to be donated to the Quebec Cystic Fibrosis Association.

The first number was the "Voices That Care" video, featuring Céline and many other internationally recognizable musicians. The audience was already on its feet, lighters glowing in the dark. The second song, "Delivre-moi" ("Deliver Me"), drew an ovation. From then on, it was two hours of happy pandemonium.

Céline was wearing one of her sexiest outfits. She thanked her songwriters, Eddy Marnay, Diane Juster, Luc Plamondon, Marcel Lefebvre, and her mom. "In my book, she's the greatest, the one who began it all."

For her first encore, she bounced back onto the stage wearing a Montreal Canadiens hockey jersey and carrying a Quebec flag. The Forum went wild. The audience started doing the wave and singing a traditional ballad to Céline.

BEAUTY AND THE BEAST

Céline and René were in London when Chris Montan, musical director at Walt

Disney Productions, called them with an offer. Disney was working on a new animated film. It was sure to be a hit, he said. Céline was the one they wanted to sing the film's theme song.

"Beauty and the Beast" would become Céline's signature song and would establish her firmly in the top echelon of the major leagues. With it, Céline would hit the home run Angélil had always predicted. Things were heating up.

March 29, 1992. Céline was in rehearsal at Ocean Way Studios, in Los Angeles. "Beauty and the Beast," the song she'd be singing with Peabo Bryson at the following day's Academy Awards gala, was a full-scale production number.

The day after, Monday, March 30, was her 24th birthday. Céline sang the duet at the Dorothy Chandler Pavilion, to more than 2,400 motion picture industry professionals and stars.

She was at a turning point in her life, and she knew it. There she was, singing with Peabo Bryson on a Hollywood

Céline is shown here with (from right to left) Mila Mulroney, Princess Diana, Prince Charles, and Canadian Prime Minister Brian Mulroney, in 1991 following a command performance for the Prince and Princess. After the show, Céline and René spent a few hours with the royal couple.

stage, in the spotlight, while the celebrities she'd always admired, the people she used to watch and dream of becoming, looked on. Just yesterday she could only dream of meeting Barbra Streisand, Elizabeth Taylor, Paul Newman, and all the other greats. And now, there they were as she sang, watching her, listening to her, standing up to applaud when she finished singing—and when "Beauty and the Beast" won the Oscar for Song of the Year.

She'd stepped through the looking glass, just like Alice in Wonderland. She was astonished, still overwhelmed by the very people who applauded her that evening.

○   ○   ○   ○   ○

On April 29, 1992, in Los Angeles, Céline and René spent a few hours by their hotel pool. That night they were scheduled to leave for New York. René

went up to his room complaining of a backache. Céline called him a bit later and his voice was weak. She hurried up to the room and immediately realized he was in trouble. He was confused and out of breath. The hotel staff helped Céline take René to an ambulance. When they reached the emergency room of Cedars-Sinai hospital, Céline saw the look on the face of the young physician who ordered René admitted to the coronary intensive care unit, and she knew his situation was critical.

René recovered quickly, and a few weeks later, when they returned to Montreal, journalist Michèle Coudé-Lord asked Céline, "You almost lost your second father, didn't you?" "Not at all," she replied. "My father is my father, and I've only got one. He protects me, encourages me, he loves me, and I love him. René is my heart. He's the one who makes it beat." For the first time, almost explicitly, she was speaking of René as the man she loved. She added that she trusted people to respect her private life. "I've got a treasure that's mine alone. I'm ready to share everything else. But not that."

○   ○   ○   ○   ○

At the Christmas holidays, René received a call saying that Céline had been nominated for a Grammy in several categories: Female Pop Vocalist of the Year, "Beauty and the Beast" was nominated for Song of the Year in the duet and pop group categories, and *Unison* was in the running for Best Album of the Year.

The Grammy gala was held on February 24, at the Shrine Auditorium in Los Angeles. Since it was impossible to award 80 prizes during the televised gala, some had been handed out earlier in the day, including Céline and Peabo Bryson's Grammy for theme song of the year. But k.d. lang won for Best Female Vocalist, and Eric Clapton won for both Best Song and Best Album.

THE 1993 JUNO AWARDS

In 1993, Dave Charles was president of the Canadian Academy of Recording Arts and Sciences, the organization that stages the Junos. Charles wanted the ceremony, televised by the CBC, to be as successful, and to create the same kind of buzz, as the Quebec Music Awards. The organizers asked Céline Dion to host the 1993 gala. She was in the running in seven categories, an all-time record.

She kicked off the ceremony with "Love Can Move Mountains," backed by a high-powered choir, Kaleefah. As host, she was direct, relaxed, warm, and quick to laugh. When she won the Juno for Female Vocalist of the Year, she thanked Angélil and, in her native French, told her parents and Quebec fans how much she loved them.

○　　○　　○　　○　　○

On March 30, her 25th birthday, she traveled to New York to see Dr. Riley, her voice coach. Everything was fine, he told her, and prescribed two days of silence. When she returned in the afternoon, René was waiting for her at Dorval Airport. In the limousine, Céline told him that, on doctor's orders, she would be keeping quiet for the next two days. Her voice had to be in shape for April 2, when she would make another landmark performance in her career.

René convinced her to switch off her voice a few hours later than she planned. He'd reserved a suite at the Four Seasons Hotel and ordered a candlelight dinner for two, accompanied by a baroque

Céline thrilled her audience with a rendition of "Love Can Move Mountains," with back-up vocals by the high-powered choir Kaleefah, at the 1993 Juno Awards celebration.

quartet. He was nervous and tense. During the meal he pulled a small box from his pocket and placed it on the table, between them. He told Céline that he loved her deeply, as he'd never loved anyone in his whole life. She opened the box, saw the ring, and broke into tears. At last their love would be known.

○   ○   ○   ○   ○

Céline inaugurated the new Theatre at the Montreal Forum on April 2, 3,

Céline, René, and a group of Chinese dancers at a benefit for Cystic Fibrosis on May 16, 1996. Ever since Céline's niece, Karine, was diagnosed with the disease, promoting awareness of CF and helping to raise funds to be used for finding a cure have been priorities in Céline's life. She works tirelessly in her efforts to help raise money for children's charities.

and 4 with French songs from *Dion chante Plamondon,* and her two English albums, *Unison* and *Céline Dion.* The show won praise, even from her usual detractors, but Angélil disagreed with the critics. He didn't like the show. Céline seemed distracted and off balance. She hadn't really touched people deeply, he said. Of course, they applauded. But she hadn't shaken them. "She's tired, I must be pushing her too hard."

Céline reassured him. No, she wasn't tired. Physically, she was in top shape. But she was worried. She could see that her niece Karine did not have

long to live. The young girl was at the Forum to witness the triumph of her aunt, her friend, her idol. But she was dangerously weak. Céline sent a limousine to Sainte-Justine hospital to pick her up. Karine came escorted by a physician and two nurses. They also carried the two oxygen bottles she was connected to.

A month later, on May 3, 1993, Karine died in Céline's arms. It was early afternoon and she'd just arrived from London. She hurried to Sainte-Anne-des-Lacs for a shower and a change of clothes, then rushed to the hospital.

Céline went to Karine, who seemed resigned to her death. "I've been waiting for you," she said to Céline. They'd given her morphine. She asked to be changed into fresh pajamas. René hurried out, found a clothing store open on Sundays, and bought three pairs.

At the hospital, Liette and Céline helped Karine change into her new pajamas. Then Céline took her in her arms, sang a French lullaby "Les Oiseaux du bonheur" ("The Birds of Happiness"), and talked to her in a soft voice.

❝*Karine started naming all the things she loved in life. Very specific things: the dinners my mother used to cook, two or three of my songs, the river, her favorite dresses. It was like an inventory, a kind of testament, a list of memories, as if she wanted to take the few beautiful things she'd known in life with her. Then she died. She was 16.*❞

TRUE LOVE REVEALED

At 25, Céline was truly happy. Her talent was hers to wield.

The night *The Colour of My Love* was launched, she announced that she was going to marry René Angélil. It had become an open secret. But her confession had an impact. People in the Métropolis Theatre in Montreal were touched. At last, life and the fiction of her songs were meeting.

She sang 7 of the album's 15 love songs, including "The Colour of My Love." The song ended with a thunderous ovation. With the final chords, Angélil stepped onto the stage and walked over to her. A tear slid down her cheek. She wiped it away. Then she took Angélil's chin in her left hand kissed him. Shouting and applause erupted, and the giant screen showed the kiss in close-up. It was almost as if they were married that night at the Métropolis Theatre, in front of 2,500 guests, and viewers from two television networks.

LIKE A FAIRY TALE

When Céline and René finally announced that they wanted a church wedding, tongues wagged furiously in countless living rooms—and in the Quebec media. Could the twice-divorced Angélil even be married in a church? Not only did Céline and René want a church wedding, they wanted a grand wedding—a fairy-tale wedding.

That summer, Céline went shopping for her bridal gown. She knew she would be coming in for criticism, but she wanted a gown with a long train: a bejeweled, spectacular gown with a wasp waist and frills and flounces. Her pumps and corset were handmade in Paris. The wedding band was created by Mauboussin, a jeweler in the Place Vendôme. She chose a heavy tiara that took all the ingenuity Louis Hechter, Céline's longtime coiffeur, could muster to find a way to keep it in place and adapt to her hairpiece.

○   ○   ○   ○   ○

Céline and René spent the evening of December 16 in the Carmelite convent in Montreal, praying. From the limousine that was driving him home, René called Francine Chaloult, his press attaché and friend. "Nothing can touch us now. Whatever may come, we're happy." Francine shared their joy.

The next day, the weather was cold. At dawn, light snow began falling on the city. It was a lovely sight. But it made it impossible to lay down carpets on the steps leading up to the church. A wooden passageway was hastily built and kept dry. The snow finally stopped less than an hour before the ceremony, which was to begin at 3:00. The wooden ramp was in place, and over it a royal blue carpet with the letters C and R in gilt. Céline's feet would be dry as she entered the church.

Shortly before 3:00, a convoy of limousines left the Westin Hotel with a police motorcycle escort. Place d'Armes in Old Montreal and the area in front of the Notre Dame Cathedral were thick

Above and below right: *In a wedding to top all weddings, Céline Dion and René Angélil were happily united in front of hundreds of family, friends, fellow artists, and international luminaries on December 17, 1994, in Montreal's Notre Dame Basilica. After years of hiding their love from the public, the two made their union official in grand fashion at their fairy-tale wedding.*

with people. Public figures such as former Canadian prime minister Brian Mulroney and his wife, Mila, David Foster, and Luc Plamondon were heartily cheered.

René was surrounded by his best men: his brother André, his cousin Paul Sara, his friends Marc Verreault, Vito Luprano, Pierre Lacroix, Guy Cloutier, Ben Kaye, and Jacques Desmarais. A few moments later, when Céline swept in on her father's arm, followed by her maids of honor, her eight sisters all in white, the church rang with cheers, shouts, and sobs. The image of Céline making her entrance into Notre Dame Basilica with her sisters holding her bridal train, wearing her white mink bolero and her jewel-studded tiara, will long remain part of the Quebec pop pantheon.

The decor was as brilliant as it was magnificent. Technicians from Solotech, the people who handled Céline's touring shows, had fine-tuned the lighting and

sound. When the Montreal Jubilation Gospel Choir broke into song, Céline, René, and a host of others were in tears.

Everything was true to their image as a couple. Flamboyant, larger-than-life, unique. The hotel's interior had been decorated to make the guests feel they were somewhere else, outside of space and time. It was a dizzying, heady sensation. Some of the decor was pure surrealism, such as the section of floor covered with flower petals, its walls hung with the finest silks embroidered with gems, or the all-white loggia—walls, floor, ceiling—where pure-white doves fluttered in white cages. From a scene straight out of *Arabian Nights* guests stepped into an English pub, from a western bar to a tiny Parisian bistro. On one counter there was sushi, on another, tapas. Magicians pulled aces of hearts from the guests' sleeves, the

champagne flowed. Everywhere there was music. A string quartet here, a rock band there. There was a casino, of course, complete with blackjack tables and roulette wheels. The money was fake, but not the winners. They were for real.

Nothing could have prepared the guests for the banquet. Bouquets of flowers came floating down from a starry sky to land softly in the center of each table. Crooner Warren Wiebe, flown in from Los Angeles for the occasion, sang "The Colour of My Love" accompanied by a 30-piece orchestra directed by David Foster. The wedding cake consisted of 2,677 cream puffs in the shape of a Christmas tree. Emotions were close to the breaking point when Céline's 13 brothers and sisters gathered around the bride to sing "Qu'elle est belle, la vie!"

Quebec had never seen another wedding ceremony like it.

LET THE GAMES BEGIN

On July 19, 1996, Céline was to sing at the opening ceremony of the Atlanta Olympic Games. The potential audience was estimated at four billion people. Half the human race. It was an enormous challenge. For her, and for René.

That afternoon she rehearsed in front of 85,000 people with the huge choir that was to accompany her. When she took the stage, she said a few words and made the crowd laugh.

Ten thousand athletes and 15,000 media representatives from around the

"THE POWER OF THE DREAM"

"APPEARANCES ASIDE, IT'S NOT AN EASY SONG TO LIKE. AS I WAS SINGING, I KEPT WONDERING JUST HOW POWERFUL DREAMS REALLY ARE. CAN YOU REALLY SUCCEED IN THIS WORLD BY WANTING AND DREAMING? THE TRUTH IS THAT FOR LOTS OF PEOPLE, IT'S NOT LIKE THAT AT ALL. SOME PEOPLE DON'T HAVE THE LUCK, THE SKILL, THE TALENT. SOME KIDS ARE BORN HEALTHY, SOME ARE BORN SICK OR CRIPPLED. SOME PEOPLE HAVE THE BODY OF AN ATHLETE, OTHERS DON'T. I WONDERED WHAT KARINE WOULD HAVE THOUGHT OF THIS SONG. WHAT WOULD THE KIDS WHO LIVE IN POVERTY IN INDIA, IN HAITI, OR IN AFRICA, OR IN THE GHETTOS OF ATLANTA AND LOS ANGELES THINK ABOUT IT?

"WHEN YOU GET RIGHT DOWN TO IT, DREAMS CAN CARRY YOU IF YOU'VE ALREADY GOT WHAT IT TAKES TO SUCCEED. THIS IS THE STORY OF MY LIFE, IN A WAY. I HAD EVERYTHING I NEEDED. I HAD A VOICE, I HAD RENÉ. AND LIKE EDDY MARNAY USED TO SAY, I WAS BORN UNDER A LUCKY STAR. BUT I HAD A DREAM OF MY OWN. I DREAMED, AND I STILL DREAM, OF SINGING ON THE WORLD'S GREATEST STAGES. BEFORE MY WEDDING [MY FRIEND] MIA COLLECTED ALL KINDS OF QUOTES FOR ME. ONE OF THEM WAS FROM CHARLES DE GAULLE. I'VE NEVER FORGOTTEN IT: 'GLORY COMES ONLY TO THOSE WHO HAVE ALWAYS DREAMED OF IT.' I CAN SAY THAT I DREAMED OF MY OWN GLORY.

"I KNOW RENÉ TOLD EVERYBODY THAT I WASN'T AFRAID. THAT'S NOT TRUE. I WAS AFRAID. GOING ONSTAGE IN A HUGE STADIUM IS ALWAYS TERRIFYING. IT'S LIKE JUMPING OFF A CLIFF. FUNNY THING, THE MORE PEOPLE THERE ARE, THE HIGHER THE CLIFF. I WAS AFRAID, BUT I WANTED TO IGNORE MY FEAR. IT ONLY REALLY HIT ME THE DAY AFTER. AFTERWARDS, I WAS SCARED TO DEATH. IT CAME IN SPURTS. FLASHES. IT TOOK ME TWO MONTHS TO WORK IT OUT OF MY SYSTEM."

world gathered in Atlanta for the Games. The song that Céline was to sing, "The Power of the Dream," is a straightforward tune, right for the circumstances. It praises the virtues of solidarity, perseverance, blind faith in the future, and faith in a world where anyone can succeed if they really want.

In the afternoon, after the rehearsal, she talked to her mother. Mrs. Dion did everything she could to conceal how nervous she was. She had decided to watch her daughter that night from their house in Sainte-Anne-des-Lacs rather

Céline and René met President Clinton at the Atlanta Olympic Games in 1996. As part of an elite jet set, they have met many of the world's most famous names.

than in Atlanta. Of course, the performance was flawless.

○   ○   ○   ○   ○

On September 20, the "Falling into You" tour kicked off in Europe with five shows in six days at Paris' Bercy Arena, a hall that holds 12,000 people. On September 20, even though the show had been going well and the crowd seemed more than satisfied, Céline felt remote, far away, distracted. "Don't worry about it," René told her. The next evening, as she left the stage, she felt pain in her stomach.

On October 1, when she taped the *Taratata* show in Paris, she was still looking wan. In Nîmes, in Le Mans, in Caen, the pain was still there. No sooner did she step onstage than it abated, and no sooner did the show end than it was back again. She managed to forget it for a few hours. The fall tour of Europe turned out to be a cure. On October 21, in the Lear jet flying them from Hamburg to Amsterdam, she turned sud-

denly to Suzanne Gingue, her tour director, and her sister Manon, as if she'd been stung by a bee. She just realized she felt no pain anywhere. It was gone. She sought it out deep inside herself. Not a trace.

From that moment on, the tour took off like a rocket. Copenhagen, Stockholm, Oslo, Berlin, Milan, Lausanne, Zurich. Never before had the musicians had so much fun playing with her. Every night she set the boards ablaze. Her voice was strong, solid. Never had her contact with the public been so warm. Everyone—Céline and the band members, the technical crew, Manon, Suzanne, and Barry Garber—lived in a kind of euphoria that fall.

On Valentine's Day, 1997, she wrote René a love letter. She doesn't like writing, or reading for that matter. "It's so complicated, and it takes so long. What counts is the intention. That's what I have to say."

❝ *My treasure, I'd love to make myself into a Queen of Hearts for the occasion. I count the days, the shows, the nights, and the hours that keep me from you. I've burned so many candles projecting your face on the walls of my hotel rooms like shadow puppets. And leaving some of my wildest dreams behind me. In the sky above my bed, every night I play the silent film in black and white, where the King meets his Queen of Hearts. They snuggle up against each other. Until they become one. How happy they are. For Valentine's Day, and for all eternity, I adore you, Your wife, Céline* "

Meanwhile her crew was hard at work on the last leg of the "Falling into You" tour, which would wind up in June in the largest venues in Europe.

○   ○   ○   ○   ○

On a frosty morning in late February, her jet hit the tarmac in New York. It had been a long flight from the Far East via Alaska. She was going to do a show—for the one and only man of her life, whom she hadn't seen for more than three weeks.

The entire day and night were devoted to him. She saw no one else. Then her public appearances began. Starting with the Grammy Awards ceremony at Madison Square Garden, a little getaway in the middle of the "Falling into You" tour. Then came the rehearsals, the interviews, the song "All By Myself" that she performed with David Foster. There was an appearance on *The Late Show* with David Letterman the next evening, where she sang "Natural Woman," then a segment on *Good Morning America* a few hours later where, for the first time on television, she performed "Fly," the English version of Jean-Jacques Goldman's "Vole." Then, the taping of an hour-long special for the BBC with the venerable George Martin, the man who produced every single Beatles record. And last, there was a meeting with the people from

Sony. All this in 48 hours. And with 11 hours worth of jet lag in her system.

New York is a brutal, in-your-face kind of town. Encountering it can be harrowing the first couple times. Céline is used to its particular effervescence, its manic disorder. The limousine came to a stop in the heavy rush-hour traffic, right under a huge poster: "Hottest tickets in AC. Tony Bennett, Tom Jones, Céline Dion."

Her tiny Madison Square Garden dressing room was crowded and overheated. Céline signed her autograph on the back of someone's guitar. The cameras moved in, focused on her, brutal and demanding. Her U.S. press attachés, Ellen and Kim, kept track of the time allocated to each journalist, and when time was up they cut off the interview and moved on.

A young lady thrust her microphone toward Céline and asked her why she sings love songs, nothing but love songs. She was intimidated, but proud of her question, which promptly set the dressing room on edge. Céline answered that love is what makes the world go round. Love is what people want to hear about and will always want to hear about. "Love songs are always in style. People need them, especially these days. Don't you think so?"

With *D'eux* and *Falling into You*, Céline Dion became, beyond a doubt, the world's top-selling singer for the previous year. She had one Grammy in her pocket already. The prize for Best Pop

Céline was honored with two Grammy Awards in 1997—Album of the Year and Best Pop Album for Falling into You.

Album of the Year had been given off air, earlier in the afternoon.

Céline had also been nominated for Best Female Vocal Performance for "All By Myself," Song of the Year for "Because You Loved Me," and Album of the Year for *Falling into You.*

Toni Braxton claimed the Grammy for Best Female Pop Vocal Performance for "Unbreak My Heart." In the Song of the Year category, "Because You Loved Me" was up against "Give Me One Reason" by Tracy Chapman, Eric Clapton's "Change the World," "Ironic" by Alanis

Morissette, and "1979" by the Smashing Pumpkins. The prize went to Clapton.

No one in Céline's entourage believed *Falling into You* was in the running for Album of the Year. But after the albums nominated for the award were announced, and the winner named, the most prestigious Grammy of them all, the most coveted, had indeed gone to *Falling into You.*

THE FAST LANE

For ten years Céline Dion has been living in the fast lane. But there are still times when things get faster. The last two weeks of March 1997 is a spectacular example.

On the night of March 18, she sang at the Orlando Arena in Florida. Then she took a helicopter to the Disney World studios, where she taped two songs for the CBC special benefit for the Quebec Cystic Fibrosis Association. At 2:00 that morning, the helicopter carried her to the airport, where she boarded the Sony jet that would carry her to Chicago. In bed at 5:00 in the morning. Up at 8:00. An hour later she joined Oprah Winfrey's talk show.

Taping began around noon. For all her fatigue, Céline talked, laughed, and made Oprah and the studio audience laugh too. Her answers to Oprah's questions were graceful and humorous. She reached out, took her hostess's hands, and asked her to talk about her own loves and dreams.

Céline sang "Because You Loved Me." In front of René. Usually when she

---

UPBEAT AND PERSONAL

In her interviews and remarks to the audience from the stage, Céline makes it clear that she is a happy person. In her field, people like her are becoming a real rarity. No complaints, no regrets, no self-pity. Quite the opposite. When she speaks of her childhood, she remembers the joys of being a little girl. For Céline Dion, life is beautiful. It always has been. But she knows that with the passage of time the people she loves will disappear, that she'll be sad, even brokenhearted.

does a television show, he stays in the control room or in front of a monitor. Today, she was a bit thrown off when she spotted him in the studio audience, in the first row. But she looked him straight in the eye and sang only for him. He was moved; everybody could see it. So was Oprah. Then Oprah sprang a surprise on Céline.

❝I was expecting an appearance by David Foster, or maybe Diane Warren, who wrote the song. When I saw my dad and mom come on stage, I just about fell off my chair. And behind them came Michel, Ghislaine, Daniel, Clément, Linda, even Louise, who came all the way from Sept-Iles. The only one missing was Claudette, who was in Barbados. When I spotted Liette I just about broke down. I was supposed to sing "Fly," the English version of "Vole." I knew that if I let myself cry, the show would be over then and there. I could never sing Karine's song in front of her mother. So I kept myself under control.❞

All together, they sang "Ce n'était qu'un rêve." Then, as she sang "Fly," she saw a stagehand guide Liette to a seat directly in front of her, right beside the camera. It was all she could do to keep going, but she did. As she sang, big

Left: *Oprah Winfrey and Céline Dion are two of the most admired women in show business. Oprah was so overjoyed with Céline's presence on her show that she canceled the guest that was to follow Céline so she could spend more time with her on camera.* Below: *Céline appeared on the* Oprah Winfrey Show *on March 19, 1997. As a wonderful surprise for Céline, her entire family flew in for the taping. "When I saw my dad and mom come on stage, I just about fell off my chair,"* Céline says. All of her brothers and sisters were there, except Claudette, who was out of the country. All together, the family sang a French folk song, wowing the studio audience and Oprah as well.*

close-ups of her and her sister alternated on the screen. Liette stifled her tears until midway through the song. At the end, Oprah herself was weeping. So were René, Michel, Liette, and most of the people in the audience. Not Céline. She couldn't let herself be overcome with emotion.

During the last commercial break, Oprah asked her if her family knew any other songs. In front of millions of American television viewers, Céline and her family sang a French folk song. Before the song, Céline related how, when she was 12 or 13, she sang songs in English without knowing what the words meant. And now, she and her family were going to sing a song that no one in the audience would understand. The audience was delighted.

After the show, Céline had only 30 minutes to talk to her folks. She was leaving for Los Angeles, where she was to record "Because You Loved Me" with a full orchestra. The song had been nominated for an Oscar. All in all, she spent less than 12 hours in Chicago.

ON TOP OF THE WORLD

Céline was in her room getting dressed and finishing her makeup for her appearance at the 1997 Academy Awards when the phone rang. Natalie Cole, in Montreal, had a bad case of the flu. She was scheduled to sing "I Finally Found Someone," the song from the film *The Mirror Has Two Faces,* starring Barbra Streisand. They had 24 hours to come up with a replacement.

"I think I can do their song," Céline told René.

He took her in his arms. "You'd better use a music stand," he suggested.

"And seated on a stool. Great idea! Besides, I do 'Because You Loved Me' standing."

No one had ever sung twice at the Oscars. Never once in 69 years. But Gil Kates, the producer of the Oscar extravaganza, loved the idea. And he wanted it to be a secret.

Céline hadn't seen Streisand's movie, nor had she heard the song. But she knew her voice, her repertoire, her favorite keys. She knew she'd like it. To her and René, Streisand was the world's greatest singer. René asked the chauffeur to stop at a record store, where they bought the soundtrack from the movie. Céline listened to "I Finally Found Someone" three or four times, her eyes closed. Streisand had recorded it as a duet with Bryan Adams.

Back at the hotel, she listened to the song again. As she did the next day, when she got up.

On Sunday afternoon, she was back in Paramount Studios to pre-record "I Finally Found Someone" just as she'd recorded "Because You Loved Me." She'd gone over it time and again in her head. She knew the song perfectly. Every note, every shading she wanted to give her voice. The musicians gave her an ovation.

On Monday evening, when they entered the Shrine Auditorium, René was looking from side to side, spotting the stars of showbiz and movies, naming them in a loud voice. "Look, there are the Coen brothers…Quentin Tarantino, Tom Cruise and Nicole Kidman…."

A few moments earlier, in the limo, they heard on the radio that Barbra Streisand was going to attend the ceremony. The idea of singing in front of her idol, especially singing a song she would perform for the first time, terrified Céline. "I see her," whispered René. "To the left, two rows behind us, just behind Muhammad Ali."

Later, as Céline took the stage to sing "Because You Loved Me," René turned to look at Streisand. But in the darkness he could not make out her features. He wanted to know what she was thinking. What was she feeling when she heard Céline sing? She must have known that Céline would also be singing her song.

During the fourth commercial break, as Céline was getting up to sing "I Finally Found Someone," René noticed that Streisand was leaving the hall. If she stayed out for more than three minutes, she would miss Céline. The doors were kept closed tight when the show was on. Why was she walking out? Before she returned, the lights dimmed. Barbra had not returned to her seat. René was doubly disappointed because Céline had sung "I Finally Found Someone" beautifully.

When Streisand returned to her seat James Brolin, her then-fiancé, leaned over and whispered in her ear. She tapped her forehead with her hand, visibly annoyed.

At a ceremony like the Oscars, the commercial breaks are always a scene of intense activity. With the cameras turned off, people get up, greet and congratulate one another, shed a few tears of discouragement or joy.

Someone touched Céline's shoulder. She turned and saw, behind James Brolin, Barbra Streisand looking at her with a big smile and extended arms. Céline went to her. Barbra took her by both hands and said, "You sing beautifully. I really love what you do."

A few minutes later, Madonna's song from *Evita,* "You Must Love Me," won the Oscar. But Céline was still the big winner in the 1997 edition of the Oscars.

❍   ❍   ❍   ❍   ❍

The day following the Oscars, Céline returned to her tour, but she insisted that René check into a health spa for a few days. A bare two hours after he checked in, René got a call from Marty Erlichman, Barbra Streisand's manager. He wanted to make sure Céline and René understood that, contrary to what the scandal sheets were saying, she hadn't walked out of the Shrine Auditorium to avoid hearing Céline, but because she really had to go to the ladies room. In fact, she was sorry she missed the performance. Angélil told Erlichman how much Céline admired Barbra, and that she dreamed of doing a song with her one day.

At almost the same time, in her suite at the San Francisco Ritz-Carlton, Céline received a huge bouquet, with a handwritten note from Barbra:

> **"***I watched the tape of the show afterwards. And you sang my song beautifully. Thank you. I only wish I had been in the room to hear it. Next time, let's do one together. P.S. I thought your song should have won. You are an incredible singer.***"**

René realized that Céline had truly become a superstar, a planetary pop diva hundreds of times bigger than anything they'd ever imagined. In early April, at the New York Marriott Marquis, she appeared in a benefit concert organized by Toys 'R' Us to raise funds for research into children's diseases. Among all the stars of American politics, sports, and motion pictures, she was the center of attention. At the airport Arnold Schwarzenegger and Maria Shriver, who were also waiting for their private jet, came over to greet her and tell her how much they loved *Falling into You*.

Céline has reached a point where there are no more models, no more signposts. She's all alone at the summit. Her voice is heard at the far corners of the world, in palaces and in slums, in streets, schools, and prisons—her image is everywhere.

"Céline was born under a lucky star," Eddy Marnay used to say. "Whatever she wanted, she had. Or she will have."

Falling into You did so well—selling more than 30 million copies around the world—that it was obvious she would make more albums. There was a new album planned for November, and a French album that Jean-Jacques Gold-

When French singer-songwriter Jean-Jacques Goldman heard Céline's voice for the first time, he was overwhelmed. "Her voice touched me. I tried my best to keep track of her. . . . At the risk of stating the obvious, there's something very special about Céline Dion. She sings, and people listen. That's what I find fascinating about her. Not only the power of her voice, not only its timbre, no matter how gorgeous it is. But the way she has of touching you to the heart." For years, whenever he was asked whose voice he would like to write for, Jean-Jacques Goldman named Céline Dion. In 1994, he finally wrote an album for her.

man was preparing for the fall of 1998. The "Let's Talk About Love" tour would wrap up on the eve of the millennium.

○   ○   ○   ○   ○

At the end of September, Céline Dion in New York and Barbra Streisand in Los Angeles listened simultaneously, via satellite, to the duet "Tell Him." They'd recorded it at different times and in different places. Barbra had recorded her part first on a blank track, without having heard Céline's part, which was to be recorded a few days later.

After the playback, a tense silence swept over the studio. Everyone was watching the telephone. It seemed to take an eternity, but it finally rang. A technician lifted the receiver and handed it to Céline. It was Barbra, calling from the other side of the continent to say how much she liked Céline's interpretation, how harmoniously she'd blended their voices.

"How do you do it?" she asked. "Your voice is like a butterfly, it's so agile and light. And then it's like a bird that flies so high no one can touch it."

Céline replied that she worked hard like an athlete, every day.

She felt like she was all alone in the studio. She'd forgotten there was anyone else there.

"You'll have to teach me how," said Barbra.

"Teach you my routine?"

"No. To discipline myself."

"But there's nothing I can teach you.

You're the greatest singer in the world."

"We can all learn something from one another. But you're a faster learner than any of us. Because you've got a great voice, and a great soul. I'm so proud of you, Céline."

66 *That's when I started to cry. I knew it was going to be a violent outburst, a regular electrical storm of tears. I wanted to tell Barbra that, for me, she was a sister. That while I was singing I felt our voices so close you couldn't tell them apart. I didn't know who I was anymore. I couldn't tell which voice was mine. I wanted to tell her all that.* **99**

Overcome with emotion, Céline handed the phone to René.

"You were always Céline's idol. She really thinks the world of you."

"I understand," said Barbra. "I felt the same way when I sang with Judy Garland. She'll get over it, let me assure you."

Céline counts Barbra Streisand as a major influence in her career. In March 1997, Céline realized a dream when she sang one of Barbra's songs, "I Finally Found Someone" from the movie The Mirror Has Two Faces, *at the Academy Awards ceremony in Los Angeles.*

Céline is pictured here with (left to right) songwriter Tony Renis, renowned opera singer Luciano Pavarotti, and record producers David Foster and Humberto Gattica.

Then she asked to speak to Céline again.

"I want to get to know you better," she said. "Come visit me in Malibu as soon as you can. Tomorrow, if you can make it."

But the next day, a Friday, Céline would be working on "I Hate You, Then I Love You" with Luciano Pavarotti. And on Saturday night, she and René were invited to his Manhattan home for dinner. They agreed on the following Tuesday.

"I'll show you my rose garden," said Barbra, "and we'll go walking on the beach."

" *Imagine being invited to dinner by your idol. Imagine her taking you in her arms. That was a great moment of happiness for me. Mind you, it's always scary to meet your idol face to face.*

You're not sure how to act. And you don't want to turn your back on the people you used to idolize.
It's like with my dreams. Everything is happening so fast. Sometimes they come true even before I've had time to really dream them.
No one wants to live without idols and without dreams. Including me. I wouldn't do it for anything in the world. **"**

For most people, dreams and real life are two separate worlds. For Céline Dion and René Angélil, those two worlds have become one. They've worked long and hard to make their dreams come true. They've been carried away by the raging torrent that their ambition has unleashed. It's risky, exciting, troubling, and thrilling. But most of all, it's loving.

The "Falling into You" Tour

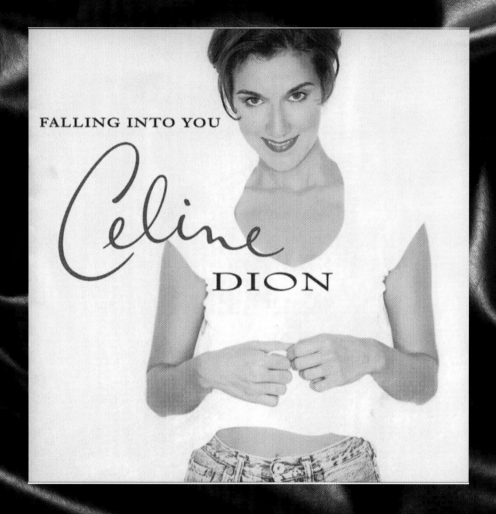

IN MARCH 1996, CÉLINE DION KICKED OFF A WORLD TOUR THAT WOULD WIND THROUGH NUMEROUS CITIES AND COUNTRIES AND EXTEND WELL INTO 1997. SHE PACKED CONCERT HALLS AND STADIUMS, FULFILLING HER WISH TO TOUCH THE HEARTS OF HER FANS ALL OVER THE GLOBE. THE "FALLING INTO YOU" TOUR SOLIDIFIED HER INTERNATIONAL FAME AND GARNERED HER MAJOR AWARDS ALL OVER THE WORLD FOR THE ALBUM OF THE SAME NAME.

The First Sigh

SHE STANDS MOTIONLESS IN THE HOT SHOWER, HER HEAD BOWED, ARMS DANGLING AT HER SIDES, WELL-BALANCED LIKE AN ATHLETE ABOUT TO JUMP OR DIVE. A THICK, WARM CLOUD OF STEAM EASES ITS FEATHERY FINGERS AROUND HER, RELAXING HER MUSCLES AND OPENING HER PORES, PULLING HER GENTLY FROM SLEEP.

SHE OPENS HER EYES AND PIVOTS HER HEAD, LEFT AND RIGHT. THE FULL FORCE OF THE SPRAY BEATS AGAINST HER FACE. THE SHOWERHEAD IS LIKE A MICROPHONE BEFORE HER. SOON, SHE WILL BREAK THE SILENCE THAT HAS ENVELOPED HER IN ITS LONELINESS FOR THE LAST 24 HOURS. TWO LONG NIGHTS AND A WHOLE DAY WITHOUT THE SLIGHTEST SOUND ISSUING FROM HER THROAT. SHE'S RESTING HER VOCAL CORDS SO THAT TONIGHT, ON STAGE IN FRONT OF 20,000 PEOPLE, HER VOICE WILL BE STRONG AND FLEXIBLE AND WILL VIBRATE—AND SET THE CROWD VIBRATING TOO.

INSIDE THE CLOUD OF STEAM, SHE CALLS UPON THE VOICE THAT'S HIDING DEEP INSIDE HER. SHE BREATHES AND SIGHS TO AWAKEN IT GENTLY. SHE PANTS, SHE MEWS, SHE GRUMBLES AND WHINES. SLOWLY, HER VOICE SPRINGS TO LIFE AND STRETCHES ITS WINGS. CLOSING HER EYES AGAIN, SHE LISTENS TO HER VOICE AS IT OVERPOWERS THE DRUMMING OF THE SHOWER, SWELLING AS IT SLOUGHS OFF THE REMAINS OF THE NIGHT.

NOW SHE'S LETTING HER VOICE RING OUT POWERFULLY TO FILL THE ROOM LIKE THE CLOUD OF STEAM THAT'S CONDENSING INTO TINY DROPLETS OF WATER ON THE WALLS AND THE MIRRORS. IT'S MUSIC NOW, VOCAL GYMNASTICS, A FINELY MODULATED MELODY. IF SHE DOESN'T HOLD BACK, HER VOICE WOULD SOAR FROM THE HOTEL WINDOW AND SWOOP HIGH OVER THE CITY, AND THE WHOLE WORLD WOULD HEAR HER SONG WITHOUT WORDS, A FRESHLY MINTED MELODY, HER OWN PURE A CAPELLA VOICE, HER VERY FIRST SIGH. BUT SHE HOLDS IT BACK. SHE KEEPS THAT SONG A SECRET, AT LEAST FOR NOW.

HER SISTER MANON, WAITING IN THE BEDROOM TO DRY HER HAIR, CAN HEAR HER VOICE. NO MORE RASPING AND HOWLING. RENÉ, WHO'S TALKING ON THE

phone or busy reading the papers or watching TV, can hear it too. She's always loved singing in the shower. The sound is clear, clean, and sharp. Like in an underground parking garage with a low ceiling where, just for fun, she might let out a whoop or two.

Her voice has been silent, held prisoner inside her, unable to speak a single word, even to René, the man she loves, the man with whom she shares everything, or to her mother, who calls every day no matter where she is. Céline answers her by tapping on the receiver with the nail of her right index finger. One tap is yes. Two means no. At the end of the conversation they send each other kisses. Sometimes they speak through Manon, who reads her sister's lips and transmits her questions and answers.

In New York, Doctor Gwen Korovin slid a tiny camera down her throat one day to show Céline her vocal chords at work. René was bewitched. "Look," he told Céline, "that's where your voice comes from." When Céline sang a few scales, they watched on the video monitor as her vocal chords swelled and contracted, touched and pressed against each other.

The doctor explained to them that the slightest contact made them stick together. Polyps could develop at those spots, tiny mucoid tumors that could grow on the vocal chords and alter her voice. Only complete and utter silence could keep those polyps from forming and leave her voice clear and powerful.

That was five years ago. Since then, Céline has learned to love the silence that at first terrorized her, as if it were a kind of emptiness that might swallow her up. Nowadays, she loves to take refuge in it. Everything seems so much more gentle in silence. Everything moves as if in slow motion: her thoughts, time, life itself. No pain and no anger can resist silence. Her voice and her ear can find peace. Her soul can be renewed.

At first, she was afraid she would forget—or talk in her sleep. Without even realizing it, the whole day's efforts would have been wasted. But she was able to follow Dr. Korovin's instructions.

She knows that René admires her and how strong, disciplined, and determined she is. He even says she's too much of a perfectionist. Maybe he's right. How could the free young girl she once was have become such a hardworking woman? She creates restrictions for herself. She takes on new obligations and challenges. René calls her an athlete, a samurai, a Marine. Sometimes she thinks he exaggerates.

She's a great pianist, Réne says, but she won't play in public because her own playing doesn't measure up to her standards. She could create original melodies and improvise like the best jazz artist, she could write songs. But she won't do it because she wants to be too perfect. He loves her for being that way. He loves her, period. He says it all the time. To everyone.

When he tells her, she tells him, "You'd better love me forever, René Angélil." She's a perfectionist, even in love—especially in love. And if he answers, "Of course, I'm going to love you for the rest of my life," she's happy, but there's sadness too. She says to herself, in a soft voice so as not to hurt him, "I wish you'd love me for the rest of *my* life, René Angélil." Because she's still young. Her life should go on for many years to come, longer than those she loves. Almost all of them are twice as old as she is. One day, probably, she'll have to live her life without them, all alone. That's the only shadow in her life. She has everything else, and a great deal of it: good health, love, fame, and fortune.

"When I think back at everything that's happened, at my life," Céline muses, "I have to admit that I've been a very lucky girl. It's incredible. The further René and I went, the better things got, the more doors opened for us. I guess I was born under a lucky star."

Getting ready to go on stage is more than hair and makeup and costumes. The crew that travels with Céline works hard to ensure that she she looks good— and that she sounds good and can put on a show that her fans will love.

She can hardly make out the reflection of her face and her slender, willowy body in the steamy mirror. She wraps her hair in a towel and slips into a big white dressing gown. Sometimes she wonders what city she's in. Stockholm, Seoul, or New York? Is this Vancouver, Hiroshima, or Milan? Montreal or Paris? For the last three years, she's lived like a nomad, always on the move, rarely spending more than four or five days in the same place. Over the last year, she has sung in countless cities in Europe, North America, the Pacific Rim, and Asia. She has lived in the most luxurious hotels these cities have to offer, in the finest suites in the world's finest palaces. The bathrooms of the finest suites of the finest hotels of the world's great cities all look alike. In Los Angeles and Prague, in Miami, Bangkok, and Berlin, you can always find marble, bronze, ceramic and porcelain, and giant mirrors. Wrapped in a cloud of steam, between four marble walls, how can she tell where she is?

She sleeps in a cool, dark room, in complete silence. At the appointed hour, usually past noon, Manon comes in to wake her without a word, without a sound, by gently stroking her foot, her hip, or her shoulders. Then she opens the curtains to let whatever remains of the streams of sunlight into the room. She lets Céline have a few precious last moments of sleep.

Manon, her sister, her confidant, her lady-in-waiting. She does her hair, grooms her, makes her laugh, tells her of the time when she was small and how her older brothers and sisters fought over who got to hold her. And she tells her where she is.

Sometimes, when they've been far from home for a long time, Manon and Suzanne Gingue, Céline's tour director, wait until she's completely awake. Then they come and lie down on the bed with her. They talk "girl talk" or look at magazines together. But most of the time, Céline prefers to face getting up alone.

On silent days, she looks at fashion or interior design magazines. She cuts out articles and photos and files them away in her scrapbooks with Manon. She designs dresses and costumes for her upcoming shows and inspects the plans for the house she's having built in Florida, near Palm Beach. Joanne, the interior decorator, sends her details of the project by fax. Then she sketches out a few ideas for another house she dreams of building in the Laurentian Mountains, north of Montreal. A great manor house with a recording studio, extra wings for her brothers and sisters and their families, a stream and a pond with weeping willows around it and wide lawns with flower beds...

She never really sees the cities where she sings. She drives through them, most often after dark, in one of those long limousines, which are the same all over the world as they glide through the streets, smelling of buffed leather. She catches a few glimpses of where she is. A street or two, a monument, a river under a bridge, sometimes a group of faces. Sometimes she doesn't even stop at the red lights. Police motorcycles escort the limousines from the airport to the hotel to the concert hall. She might not recognize the streets or buildings or city squares, but she can distinguish the people by the way they talk, and by their faces. She never feels lost among her fans. She knows exactly where she is. She can recognize the crowds by their shouts and laughter. Crowds in Asia, in Europe, or in America—she knows their reactions and their ovations. She'll do anything to charm and captivate them. That's her trade, her passion, her life's work.

This morning, she is in New York. She makes her own breakfast. Oatmeal with brown sugar, strawberry jam, toasted French bread, three helpings of stewed pears, and peanut butter. No dairy products, no carbonated beverages.

Manon will be with her everywhere she goes today, right up to the short stairway that leads to the stage where, a few hours from now, in front of 20,000 fans, Céline will let her voice ring free. And the whole world will be set free with her.

Céline has always had a great interest in fashion. The fashion world fascinates her almost as much as music. In recent years, she has become a patron of the world's top designers. She is pictured here with John Galliano, designer for Christian Dior, at the 1998 Pret-á-Porter in Paris.

Departure

I**T'S SEPTEMBER. T**HE SKIES ARE GRAY BUT THE AIR IS MILD. O**N THE UPPER FLOORS OF THE BUILDINGS THERE ARE NARROW BALCONIES WITH POLISHED IRON GRILLWORK. F**ROM TIME TO TIME, A CURTAIN MOVES IN THE TALL WINDOWS. S**OME OF THE PEOPLE IN THE CROWD ARE HOLDING CAMERAS WITH TELEPHOTO LENSES. T**HEIR CAMERAS ARE TRAINED ON THE WINDOWS OF THE HOTEL. O**THERS ARE HOLDING SMALL BOUQUETS OF FLOWERS, OR A PAD OF PAPER AND A PEN, OR AN ENVELOPE THAT CONTAINS A LETTER THEY INTEND TO PRESS INTO CÉLINE'S HAND. T**HEY HOPE TO COME AWAY WITH AN AUTOGRAPH, OR A LOOK AND A SMILE. M**AYBE THEY CAN EVEN TOUCH HER.

S**HE LOVES P**ARIS PASSIONATELY, THAT BEAUTIFUL, REFINED CITY WHERE SHE FEELS ALMOST AS MUCH AT HOME AS SHE DOES IN M**ONTREAL OR P**ALM B**EACH. S**HE'S BEEN COMING TO P**ARIS REGULARLY SINCE 1982, THE YEAR SHE RECORDED HER FIRST SONGS. P**ARIS WAS THE FIRST TO LOVE HER, AND IT HASN'T FORGOTTEN HER BEGINNINGS.

T**HE LIMOUSINES THAT WILL WHISK CÉLINE AND HER ENTOURAGE AWAY ARE PARKED UP THE STREET. T**HE DRIVERS ARE TALKING AMONG THEMSELVES, STANDING ON THE SIDEWALK. O**NE OF THEM HAS A RECEIVER IN HIS EAR AND A TINY MICROPHONE ATTACHED TO HIS RIGHT WRIST. F**ROM TIME TO TIME, HE SPEAKS QUICKLY INTO HIS HAND, THEN HE LISTENS TO THE ANSWER, EYES HALF-CLOSED IN CONCENTRATION, HIS FINGER PRESSED AGAINST THE RECEIVER IN HIS EAR. I**N FRONT OF THE HOTEL ENTRANCE, PORTERS, CAR JOCKEYS, BELLBOYS, AND MEN IN LIVERIES COME AND GO. S**OME OF THEM ARE PLUGGED IN, TOO.

E**VERY TIME THE HOTEL DOORS SWING OPEN, A MURMUR RUNS THROUGH THE CROWD. W**HEN E**RIC APPEARS, EVERYONE SENSES THAT THE TIME IS NEAR. F**ANS IN THE KNOW RECOGNIZE E**RIC B**URROWS, CÉLINE'S BODYGUARD.

E**RIC TAKES UP POSITION IN FRONT OF THE HOTEL. H**E LOOKS THE CROWD OVER. H**E KNOWS THAT CÉLINE D**ION'S FANS ARE THE NICEST IN THE WORLD. B**UT THERE'S ALSO THE PAPARAZZI—THEY'RE ALWAYS IN SEARCH OF A PHOTO THAT WILL MAKE THE STAR LOOK BAD.

The 1998 Academy Awards ceremony was no different than any other appearance for Eric Burrows, Céline's bodyguard. As at all events, he stuck close by and kept a watchful eye.

She'll be here soon. Her fans can read the signs. The chauffeurs have gotten into their cars. A limo at the foot of the street is blocking off all access. At the top of the street, police officers are getting ready to close the side streets.

First come Manon and Gilles Hacala, her companion. He looks after the

DARE TO DREAM

WHEN RENÉ ASKS CÉLINE WHAT SHE'D LIKE TO DO IF SHE HAD A YEAR OFF, SHE ALWAYS SAYS THE SAME THING. FIRST, SHE'D LIKE TO HAVE A CHILD. THEN SHE'D LEARN SPANISH AND VISIT SOME OF THE CITIES SHE TRAVELED THROUGH SO QUICKLY DURING HER TOURS. VENICE, OF COURSE. AND PRAGUE, BARCELONA, KYOTO . . . SHE'S MADE PLENTY OF PLANS. A NIGHT AT THE PARIS OPERA, ON THE ARM OF THE MAN SHE LOVES. A DINNER FOR TWO AT THE JULES VERNE RESTAURANT, HIGH ATOP THE EIFFEL TOWER, WITH ITS VIEW OF THE WINKING LIGHTS OF PARIS AND THE BLACK RIBBON OF THE SEINE RIVER. LONG WALKS THROUGH BATTERY SQUARE IN NEW YORK. SHOPPING ON THE VIA DEL CORSO IN ROME AND THE GINZA IN TOKYO. AND FOR A WHILE, SHE'D LIKE TO DO NOTHING AT ALL, IN HER HOUSE IN MONTREAL, OR IN THE LAURENTIAN MOUNTAINS NORTH OF THE CITY, OR IN PALM BEACH. BUT RENÉ LAUGHS AND TELLS HER SHE'D NEVER BE ABLE TO SIT STILL.

logistics of the tour. Céline is behind them, escorted by Eric and René. In the five or six yards between the door of the hotel and the door of the limousine, Céline will take the time to talk to several people, smile at them, touch their hands, sign three or four autographs. Eric sticks close by. Then he urges Céline and Manon into the limo. René gets in on the other side. It happens very fast. Security guards escort the car on both sides and move onlookers out of the way so the vehicles can pass quickly.

Céline has come and gone. Silence settles over the street. The fans begin to scatter.

Now the limousines are hurtling down the expressway at sunset. A ray of golden sun shines in the autumn Paris sky, then the rain returns, soft and mild.

Céline has filled the Bercy Arena in Paris four times in recent days. It's the biggest concert hall in Paris. Her mother, her father, and her Aunt Jeanne saw all four shows at the Bercy amphitheater. Céline introduced them to the crowd. "Papa! Maman!" she called, and spotlights shone upon them. Mr. Dion is more timid than his wife, and he suffers from stage fright, but he stood up and smiled and waved to the audience. Then he blew kisses to his daughter.

Céline is very much like her mother. At 70 years old, Thérèse Dion just can't stop. She works seven days a week in her restaurant outside Montreal, keeping house in Sainte-Anne-des-Lacs in the mountains, traveling around the world several times a year to see her baby sing. Céline, on the other hand, is constantly busy as part of the jet set. She's met all the world's great names: Pope John Paul II, Queen Elizabeth II of England, President Clinton, cabinet ministers, princes, the most famous fashion designers in Paris, Milan, New York, and Tokyo. She's on a first-name basis with the top show business stars in Europe and America.

It is late and the limousines are slowly driving down the tarmac at the Paris airport. They pull up next to the Lear jet. The crew is waiting by the steps. As they leave Paris, the sun sits low in the sky. The plane turns its back on it and heads for the Alps. Céline says a little prayer, as she does every time her plane takes off, her head bent, her hands crossed on her knees, her lips speaking words that only she knows. A prayer she's never told anyone, not even René. Everyone else falls silent and waits for her to finish. Tonight, Céline has the blues.

She stares out at the clouds. René had returned to Montreal two days earlier. He had business to attend to. In two days he was to receive a Félix from the Quebec Music Awards. Every year, Félix Awards are given to Quebec artists and producers in show business. This year, a special Félix Award was to be given to René for his overall achievement, for his masterpiece—Céline Dion.

Tonight, far from his side, onboard a jet cutting through the European skies,

that masterpiece has the blues. At every hour of the day or night, even when they are separated by oceans and by continents, Céline and René are in constant contact. Each one knows where the other is, and with whom, and what they're doing. René knows that Céline is traveling through the skies above Europe, and that Suzanne, Eric, Gilles, and Manon are with her, seeing to her every need. Also on the plane are Dave Platel, René's right-hand man, and Barry Garber, Céline's "Minister of Foreign Affairs," who is in charge of planning her touring activities.

It's a queen's court, a very functional family where everyone's job is to make all things as pleasant as they possibly can be. The machine must run efficiently, smoothly, and fast. Barry has arranged for Céline and her entourage to be met at the Geneva airport. Everything is ready at the Arena. The musicians came in the night before from Belgium, where Céline sang two days earlier. The technicians have set up the stage and installed the lighting board programmed by the engineers. Céline's dressing room has been decorated. There are flowers, her knickknacks, and lucky charms. The caterers are preparing the meal she'll eat this evening with the entire team . . . but without René.

Wherever she goes, Céline is sure to be recognized by admiring fans. Here, she autographs a lucky fan's tambourine outside the Four Seasons hotel in New York City.

The Press Conference

A S THE DC-8 LIFTED OFF FROM NAGOYA EN ROUTE TO SEOUL, THE PLANE BANKED SHARPLY. CÉLINE WAS SAYING HER SECRET PRAYER, AND FOR A MOMENT, THE PLANE SEEMED TO HANG MOTIONLESS IN THE AIR. THEN CAME AN INSTANT OF PANIC: HOW COULD ANYTHING THAT HEAVY STAY UP IN THE SKY? WHAT WOULD KEEP IT FROM CRASHING INTO THE WATER BELOW?

THOUGH THE FLIGHT PROCEEDED NORMALLY, CÉLINE STILL FELT NERVOUS. SHE HAD ONLY ONE DESIRE: TO TURN AROUND AND GO HOME. YET THE DC-8 OFFERED EVERY POSSIBLE LUXURY. CÉLINE HAD A SPACIOUS ROOM WITH A DOUBLE BED, A WASHROOM, AND A SHOWER. FOR THE REST OF THE TEAM, THERE WERE TWO LARGE SALONS, COMFORTABLE SOFAS, AND BUNKS. IT WAS DARK WHEN THE AIRPLANE TOUCHED DOWN IN SEOUL ON A GLISTENING, WET RUNWAY. EVERY-ONE WAS FEELING THE TENSION BY THEN.

THE AIRPORT WAS DARK AND DESERTED. COLD DRAFTS BLEW THROUGH IT. SUZANNE GINGUE, MANON, ERIC, AND DAVE PLATEL TRIED TO SHIELD CÉLINE FROM THE WIND. THE CITY WAS A HEAVY-METAL MAELSTROM. ELEVEN MILLION HUMAN BEINGS LIVED THERE. EVERYTHING SEEMED DISORGANIZED AND VIOLENT. BARRY GARBER HAD BEEN WARNED THAT THERE WOULD BE TERRIBLE TRAFFIC JAMS, AND THAT IT MIGHT TAKE THEM AN HOUR AND A HALF TO GET TO THE HILTON. AT 8:00, CÉLINE WAS TO GIVE A MAJOR PRESS CONFERENCE AT THE HOTEL.

THERE WAS BEDLAM AT THE HILTON. THE LIMOUSINES HAD TO PUSH THROUGH THE CROWD. CÉLINE HAD TO REACH THE MEZZANINE OVERLOOKING THE MAIN LOBBY, WHICH WAS JAMMED WITH EXCITED FANS WHO TURNED TO RUSH AT HER. ERIC GRABBED HER BY THE WAIST AND HEADED FOR THE ELEVATORS. IT WAS LIKE MOSES PARTING THE RED SEA. HE MANAGED TO ESCORT HER TO HER PENTHOUSE SUITE THAT STRETCHED OVER TWO FLOORS. IT AFFORDED A BREATHTAKING VIEW.

FIFTEEN MINUTES LATER, CÉLINE STEPPED INTO THE MEETING ROOM. MORE THAN A HUNDRED JOURNALISTS FROM ALL OVER THE FAR EAST HAD BEEN WAITING FOR HER FOR OVER AN HOUR.

Giving a press conference is part of Céline's job. She's learned to enjoy speaking to crowds, getting her point—and her passion—across to her listeners. Whether she's at home in Montreal, as she is here, talking about the release of her Let's Talk About Love *album, or in Seoul, Korea, with her Asian fans, Céline is able to speak from—and to—the heart.*

solation prize Sony was offering the countries that Céline hadn't had time to visit on this tour. It was also, as Martin T. Davis, vice president of Sony's operations in Hong Kong, said, a way of saluting the people of the Far East. "Céline Dion will be spending more time in Asia," he promised.

Canada's ambassador to Seoul made a short speech, presented Céline with a Team Canada sweatshirt, and declared her an honorary member of the team. Mr. Hun Bang, a native of Seoul who was involved with the producers of Céline's show, handled the translation from French to Korean.

Sony representatives from a half-dozen countries stepped forward to present Céline with platinum records. Finally, the press conference began. It was a formal affair, with a host. Anyone wanting to ask a question had to identify themselves first. There were the usual questions. The kind she'd heard everywhere for the last two years. She answered pleasantly despite her fatigue and hunger, and despite the sense of foreboding that had filled her since their takeoff from Japan.

Then, finally, a young man asked a question that had real meaning to her: "What keeps you going?" Céline stopped to think. Then she spoke of her parents, describing how hard they'd always worked, how they'd built the house they'd raised their children in, how they'd found happiness and a sense of stability in their work. "I was brought

There were banners and giant posters with the *Falling into You* album cover. Long tables had been arranged in a semicircle. Microphones and cameras represented TV stations from seven Asian countries: South Korea, Taiwan, the Philippines, Thailand, Hong Kong, Singapore, and Malaysia.

Standing at the podium, looking very slender in her gold Chanel jacket, Céline smiled as the cameras flashed. The press conference was a kind of conup that way," she added. "Besides, every time I stop working, believe it or not, I get sick. To tell the truth, the thing that motivates me and keeps me going is the need to feel good about myself. And I never feel good about myself when I'm not doing anything."

She made the reporters laugh when she admitted that she'd always believed she had a lucky star to guide her. A kind of guardian angel. She told them about her idea of happiness: traveling and seeing the world, discovering the similarities behind the many small differences. There was another kind of happiness, too, that sometimes, for no good reason, lifted up her heart and soul. "Real happiness," she said, "might have something to do with doing your job well. But it's not always earned, it's not always fair. There are some people that happiness just doesn't want to touch." That's her way of talking about her niece Karine, about cystic fibrosis and other childhood diseases that haunt her thoughts.

Someone asked her which are her favorite songs. "They're like my children," she answered immediately. "I think that my mother loved each of her 14 children with equal care and affection. The same thing goes for my songs. They all have a way of reaching out and touching people, and changing their lives sometimes. Maybe they just add a little hope and light to their day. My songs can go anywhere: into the bedroom, in the kitchen early in the morning with the smell of toast and coffee, in elevators, in cars speeding down the expressways. Music is like water. And it's like fire too. It can spread."

When Dave Platel stepped up to say the interview was over, she thanked the journalists and the people from Sony who had organized the press conference. "We have grown up together, you and I," she said. "I owe my success to you." Dead tired, she was escorted from the room as the crowd applauded heartily.

Next, she was to meet some key people from Sony. She was to put her hands on a block of plaster and sign it with a knife. The plaster had already started to harden. She was willing to try again. "A job worth doing is worth doing well," she said. But there was no more plaster. And no more time either. She had to hurry off to do a radio interview. Then there would be a photo session with some fans from Seoul who had won a contest. It was almost midnight when Dave stepped in again, politely but firmly. He tore Céline away from her fans and escorted her to the restaurant where her entourage was waiting for her. On a tour, these private moments are always reassuring.

They talked about the panic attack she'd had leaving Nagoya, and the terrible traffic jams in Seoul, and the extraordinary press conference, and the monstrously large suite where Céline would sleep, all by herself. And they talked about René, of course.

Then Céline said how much she loved him.

To the Concert Hall

AS SOON AS THE PLANE TOUCHED DOWN, GILLES HACALA TOLD THE CREW THAT CÉLINE AND HER ENTOURAGE WOULD BE AT THE CONCERT HALL IN LESS THAN 30 MINUTES. AROUND 5:00, THE CROWD OF YOUNG PEOPLE AROUND THE POINT SPOTTED THE LIMOUSINES. THEY WERE DRIVING UP THE STREET THAT RUNS ALONG THE LIFFEY, THEN THEY CIRCLED PAST THE LITTLE PARK AND SPED UP THE DRIVE INTO THE GIANT GARAGE. WITHOUT SLOWING DOWN, THE LONG BLACK CARS DISAPPEARED INTO THE ENORMOUS BUILDING WHERE THE TECHNICIANS WERE FINISHING THE STAGE SET-UP. ERIC MOVED THROUGH THE CONCERT HALL, LOOKING UNDER THE SEATS IN THE FIRST FEW ROWS, EVALUATING THE EXITS, CALCULATING THE DISTANCES. MEANWHILE, THE MUSICIANS PROCEEDED WITH THE SOUND CHECK.

IN THE GARAGE, BY THE BUSES, STOOD EIGHT TRUCKS, EACH ONE NEARLY 15 YARDS LONG. THEY HAD COME FROM LONDON WITH ALL THE TOUR EQUIPMENT, 176,000 POUNDS OF MATERIAL. FLOODLIGHTS, PROJECTORS, TAPE RECORDERS, MILES OF ELECTRICAL WIRE AND CABLES, CATHODE-RAY SCREENS, COMPUTERS, CONSOLES FOR MONITORING THE IMAGES AND FOR DOING THE SOUND MIX, LOUDSPEAKERS, SMOKE MACHINES, SPOTLIGHTS AND MICROPHONES, CAMERAS, CLOTHES, THE TECHNICIANS' AND THE MUSICIANS' BAGGAGE, GUITARS, DRUM KITS, KEYBOARDS, PLATES AND COOKING POTS, UTENSILS, TOOLS OF ALL KINDS.

WHEN THEY GET TO A NEW PLACE, THE FIRST PERSON CÉLINE AND MANON USUALLY SEE IS THEIR BROTHER MICHEL, HIS GREY HAIR PULLED BACK IN A PONYTAIL, WALKIE-TALKIE IN HAND. HE SHOWED THE DRIVERS WHERE TO PARK THEIR CARS, THEN WENT AND KISSED HIS SISTERS. MICHEL IS A REASSURING AND FAMILIAR PRESENCE. WHEN HE'S THERE, IT MEANS THAT THE DION TEAM HAS TAKEN POSSESSION OF THE CONCERT HALL. THEY CAN RELAX NOW. HE'S THE TOUR DIRECTOR'S ASSISTANT, IN CHARGE OF THE MUSICIANS AND THEIR INSTRUMENTS. HE'S THEIR SHEPHERD. THIS MORNING, HE ESCORTED THE MUSICIANS TO THEIR HOTEL, MADE SURE EVERYONE HAD THE RIGHT ROOM AND THE RIGHT SUITCASE, AND SET DOWN THE SCHEDULE FOR THE DAY. HE IS KIND AND COMPETENT.

Ever since dawn broke, The Point has been a busy construction site. The action there is positively frenetic. Seen from behind, the stage looks something like a giant ship about to set sail with its scaffolding, hanging cables, tall masts, great hull, and crisscrossing bridges and catwalks. The crew is putting on the finishing touches. Each type of technician wears a different color. The carpenters wear black T-shirts, the cameramen are in blue, the sound techs in green, and the lighting people wear yellow.

They arrived in Dublin during the night. They slept in the tour buses on the English highways, then on the Irish Sea onboard the ferry. The buses are regular houses on wheels, with living rooms both front and back, wide, comfortable sofas, music, television, beds, storage space, a library, a selection of videos, games, a microwave oven, and all anyone would want to eat and drink.

A small army of over 50 men and women from Quebec accompany Céline in her travels around the globe. They're a very close-knit group, very united and well organized. They fall into a natural hierarchy made up of three separate societies: technicians, musicians, and Céline's personal attendants. In every city and every country, support staff is added, including various suppliers and providers of services, members of the media, and drivers.

At The Point, Louise Labranche, better known as Loulou, has hung changes of clothes for Céline in a kind of tent. There's the long skirt and blouse she'll wear for her encores. Carefully folded white towels, a hairbrush, face creams, and powder. White arrows, taped to the floor, lead from Céline's dressing room to the stage. Where it is

APRIL 30, 1988
EUROVISION AWARDS

IN THE 1988 EUROVISION COMPETITION, CÉLINE WAS REPRESENTING SWITZERLAND. THE COMPETITION DRAWS MORE THAN 20 PARTICIPATING COUNTRIES EVERY YEAR AND GIVES EUROPEAN ARTISTS THE KIND OF VISIBILITY PEOPLE DREAM ABOUT. IT ENDS WITH A TELEVISED SPECIAL THAT REACHES 600 MILLION VIEWERS. IN THE PAST, THE WORLD'S TOP PERFORMERS (WHO WEREN'T ALWAYS THE WINNERS) HAD TAKEN PART: THE SWEDISH GROUP ABBA, THE SPANISH SINGER WITH THE VELVET VOICE JULIO IGLESIAS, THE GREEK SONGSTRESS NANA MOUSKOURI, AND AUSTRALIA'S OLIVIA NEWTON-JOHN. EACH PARTICIPATING COUNTRY SELECTS THE SONG THAT WILL REPRESENT IT AT THE TELEVISED GALA, HELD EVERY YEAR IN A DIFFERENT CITY, AND 1988 WAS DUBLIN'S TURN.

CÉLINE FINISHED THE PRELIMINARY ROUND WITH 48 POINTS; HER NEAREST RIVAL HAD 23. HER VICTORY WAS OVERWHELMING. ECSTATIC, ON APRIL 28, CÉLINE AND RENÉ JETTED OFF TO DUBLIN, WHERE SINGERS, PRODUCERS, SONGWRITERS, AND COMPOSERS FROM NO LESS THAN 30 COUNTRIES WERE GATHERING.

IN DUBLIN, IN THE DAYS LEADING UP TO THE EUROVISION FINALS, OPEN LEGAL BETTING WAS IN FULL SWING. OVER THE PRECEDING WEEK, CÉLINE HAD ESTABLISHED HERSELF AS ONE OF THE THREE FAVORITES. AFTER SHE APPEARED ON A LOCAL TELEVISION SHOW, SHE VAULTED INTO THE TOP SPOT. WHEN REHEARSALS GOT UNDERWAY IN THE IMMENSE SIMMONSCOURT STUDIOS, SHE WAS A 7–4 FAVORITE.

CÉLINE SANG WITH PASSION, EVEN IF HER SONG WASN'T A MASTERPIECE OF INSPIRATION. HER LONG, WAVY HAIR CASCADED DOWN OVER AN IMPECCABLY TAILORED SUIT IN HUES OF TURQUOISE AND DARK BERRY. AFTER THE 21 FINALISTS—WHOSE ORDER HAD BEEN DETERMINED IN A DRAW—HAD SUNG, THEY WITHDREW TO THE SIMMONSCOURT GREEN ROOM WHERE THEY AWAITED THE VERDICT. THE JURY, MADE UP OF EIGHT MEN AND EIGHT WOMEN OF ALL AGE GROUPS FROM SEVERAL COUNTRIES, DELIBERATED LONG AND HARD. THE FINAL SCORE WAS AS CLOSE AS IT COULD BE: SWITZERLAND 137, ENGLAND 136!

CÉLINE ALREADY HAD A STRONG HOME-TOWN REPUTATION AS A WEEPER. VICTORIES AND OVATIONS BROUGHT TEARS TO HER EYES FASTER THAN ANY DEFEAT. THERE, BEFORE THE PUBLIC AT SIMMONSCOURT AND THE 600 MILLION TELEVISION VIEWERS WATCHING THE EUROVISION GALA, SHE BROKE INTO TEARS. HER MESSAGE OF THANKS WAS AN INCOHERENT BABBLE.

Céline rehearses in Las Vegas before her performance at the 1996 Billboard Music Awards show.

too dark, glowing cables are stretched along the railing. The path that Céline will take from her dressing room to the Dublin stage will be well lit. Soon she will meet the people of the Irish capital. She loves them. They're sentimental, they have great spirit, they love the intoxication and magic of music. She loves them best of all because it was here, ten years ago, on April 30, 1988, that she won the 1988 Eurovision Awards. It had changed her career and her life.

When Céline walks into The Point, or any concert hall, emotions always run high. She's the last piece in a giant jigsaw puzzle. Most of the time, she doesn't even take off her jacket or boots. She doesn't even bother stopping at her dressing room. She goes right to the stage. She walks back and forth across it, looks over the empty hall, kisses and hugs the musicians and technicians who are doing the sound check and fine-tuning the lighting effects.

Her People

THE CAMERAMEN WHO PROVIDE THE PICTURES FOR THE ONSTAGE SCREENS KNOW THE SHOW BY HEART. EVERY NOTE OF MUSIC, CÉLINE'S EVERY MOVE, EVERY LIGHTING EFFECT. IT'S BARELY CHANGED FOR MONTHS. AT FIRST THEY HAD TROUBLE FOLLOWING HER ON STAGE. SHE WASN'T SURE OF HER STEPS, HER MOVEMENTS, HER WORDS. BUT AS TIME PASSED, EVERYTHING FELL NATURALLY INTO PLACE. NOW THE SHOW IS A WELL-OILED MACHINE, A PIECE OF PRECISION CLOCKWORK THAT NEVER LOSES A SECOND.

JUST FOR FUN, YVES AUCOIN, ALSO KNOWN AS LAPIN, PLAYED THREE DIFFERENT RECORDINGS ON THE MONITORS. THE CAMERAMEN AND THE TECHNICAL CREW WATCHED CLOSELY. IN MOST OF THE SONGS, CÉLINE'S MOVEMENTS WERE PERFECTLY SYNCHRONIZED. THE SAME MOVES AT THE EXACT SAME MOMENT.

BUT THERE ARE TIMES WHEN SHE DEPARTS FROM THE NORM. TIMES WHEN SHE'S TIRED OR NERVOUS. IN MONTREAL, EVERY SHOW IS DIFFERENT; NO ONE EVER KNOWS EXACTLY WHAT'S GOING TO HAPPEN. IT'S AS IF CÉLINE WANTS TO REDISCOVER THE CONFUSION, THE INNOCENCE, THE VULNERABILITY OF OLD TIMES. TO BE HERSELF, IN THIS CITY MORE THAN ANYWHERE ELSE. THE WAY OLD HABITS SHOULD HAVE NO PLACE WHEN TWO PEOPLE IN LOVE MEET AFTER A LONG SEPARATION. THERE'S ALWAYS A SENSE OF THE UNKNOWN, THE TANTALIZING SHYNESS.

ONE COULD ARGUE THAT, IN PURELY TECHNICAL TERMS, THE SHOW IS NOT AS GOOD IN MONTREAL AS IT IS ELSEWHERE. THERE ARE FLUBS, A FEW MINOR SLIPS, ONE OR TWO MISTAKES. BETWEEN SONGS, CÉLINE SOMETIMES STRUGGLES FOR WORDS. BUT THERE'S ALSO A DIRECTNESS, A WARMTH, A SENSE OF INTIMACY, A SPIRIT THAT'S IMPOSSIBLE TO FIND IN HER SHOWS ANYWHERE ELSE IN THE WORLD. IN MONTREAL, EVERYONE IN THE CREW IS ALWAYS ON PINS AND NEEDLES. AND, IN THE END, RARELY IS EVERYONE COMPLETELY SATISFIED. THERE'S ALWAYS THE FEELING THAT THINGS COULD HAVE BEEN BETTER, MORE MAGICAL.

ONE EVENING, AT THE MOLSON CENTER, THE CAMERAMEN WERE HAVING TROUBLE KEEPING UP WITH CÉLINE. HER MOVES WEREN'T THE SAME. THEY WERE

Céline always has time for her fans. Here, she autographs a soundtrack album from the film Titanic. *Her rendition of James Horner's "My Heart Will Go On" won an Academy Award.*

for instance. But that doesn't mean that the singer who sells the largest number of albums is the best. I'm in competition with myself. Barbra Streisand hardly gives any shows. She sells fewer records than Mariah Carey, Alanis Morissette, Whitney Houston, or me. But in my opinion, she's the greatest singer in the world. Because she's the one who can control her voice the best, who can use it to communicate emotions—not only her own, but those that are in the music, and the words she sings. "

more abrupt, less rounded. There was a faint, almost undetectable, note of nervousness in her voice.

Before the show there had been a press conference, and a few journalists had asked her questions she didn't particularly care for. Then, a little girl not more than ten years old stepped up to the mike, and in front of the entire Montreal press corps, proclaimed that she wanted to be a great singer. She asked Céline, "Would you be jealous if I became a greater singer than you?" People applauded. Céline gave the child a long answer. Basically, she explained, she wasn't in competition with anyone but herself.

" *It's true. I don't believe in competition. Every singer has her own voice. Sure, there are things you can measure. The number of albums sold,*

After this press conference, awards were handed out. And a thick knot of people gathered in front of Céline's dressing room. Just before stepping on stage, she asked to be left alone for a few moments. She and René strolled around the backstage area. The show promised to be tough and complicated. At 8:50, Céline would be broadcast live on television as she sang "It's All Coming Back to Me Now," the show's 15th song. The broadcast would be a part of a special benefit program for the amateur athletics foundation, the rest of which had been taped six days earlier at a Montreal indoor sports arena. Céline appears dressed in the Canadian Olympic uniform, diving, running, and jumping with Olympic champions Sylvie Bernier and Annie Pelletier. With them were a dozen athletes who would be leaping onto the Molson Center stage when she swung into "The Power of the Dream" backed up by the Montreal Jubilation Choir.

Her job was going to be more than a little bit complicated. And that meant pressure. Everyone in her entourage knew it was creative pressure, but it wasn't always easy to put up with.

As soon as she stepped on the stage, most of her tension evaporated. Throughout the show, which began with "J'attendais," Céline talked and laughed a lot. She was eager to let the Montrealers know that she was one of them, that she hadn't changed a bit, that she was nice and simple, just like them.

She told them how, when she came back to Montreal after being away for several months, she asked her driver to stop at a convenience store. René went in and bought some white bread, "You know, the kind that sticks to your teeth and the roof of your mouth" and sliced chicken "that doesn't taste like anything." When they got back home they made sandwiches. She talked of the pleasure of sleeping in her own bed. She wanted Quebecers to know that she missed being there.

As she sang "Love Can Move Mountains" a fan placed a small paper bag at the edge of the stage. Usually gifts start arriving much earlier in the show, during "Seduces Me" or "All By Myself." When she finished the song, everyone spotted the bag at her feet. She bent down, picked it up, peeked inside, and

exclaimed, "Good Lord in Heaven! Cookies!" She sat down on the edge of the stage in front of Marc Langis and tasted one.

Each move is perfectly choreographed and well rehearsed ahead of time, but Céline, a born performer, is able to make every show look as if it is being done expressly for the people in front of her.

"*Sure I knew René, Eric, everybody would be beside themselves. Who could tell what might be in those cookies? But I was so sure of myself, I knew nothing bad could happen to me. Sometimes I feel that way when I'm on stage. As if nothing can touch me. It's an extraordinary feeling.*"

On Stage

I N FUKUOKA, JAPAN, CÉLINE STEPPED OUT OF THE LIMOUSINE, SAID HELLO TO THE TECHNICIANS WHO WERE ALREADY HARD AT WORK, AND KISSED LOULOU, HER WARDROBE MISTRESS. THEN SHE DISAPPEARED. SHE SLIPPED INTO ONE OF THE GIANT FOLDS OF THE LARGE BLACK CURTAIN THAT PRO- VIDED THE BACKDROP FOR THE STAGE. SHE WAS PLAYING HIDE-AND-SEEK WITH MANON, MICHEL, AND LOULOU. THE MUSICIANS WERE PASSING TIME UNTIL THE SHOW BEGAN.

DOMINIQUE MESSIER STARTED IT, LAYING DOWN THE RHYTHM ON DRUMS. GENTLY AT FIRST, THEN ADDING A STRONGER BEAT. MÉGO SLIPPED IN SENSUAL PIANO PHRASINGS TO COMPLEMENT COUTU'S CHIRPY GUITAR. MARC LANGIS' HARD- HEADED BASS PROVIDED RICH GROUND FOR THEIR IMPROVISATIONS. PAUL PICARD CHIMED IN WITH PERCUSSION, AND FRULLA'S KEYBOARDS SOARED HIGH ABOVE THE OTHER INSTRUMENTS. IT WAS PURE MUSIC, WILD AND FREE, AND THE MUSICIANS WERE GIVING IT ALL THEY HAD.

JUST WHEN THE BACK-UP SINGERS WERE STARTING TO REALLY GET INTO IT, CÉLINE STEPPED FROM HER HIDING PLACE AND ADDED HER VOICE TO THEIRS. SHE WAS WEARING A LONG, SEA-GREEN CASHMERE COAT, HIGH BOOTS, AND A SCARF— NOT YET DRESSED IN THE COSTUME SHE WOULD DON FOR THE PERFORMANCE. WHEN SHE LOOKED AT THE STAGE, EVERYTHING WAS EXACTLY AS IT SHOULD BE. THEN SHE LOOKED OUT AT THE MAIN FLOOR AND THE BALCONIES; FUKUOKA'S MA- RINE MESSE SEEMED DAMP, COLD, AND SAD. EMPTY CONCERT HALLS ARE NOT VERY FRIENDLY PLACES.

THEN SHE SANG A FEW NOTES. SHE CLOSED HER EYES AND FOLLOWED THE SOUND OF HER VOICE INTO THE DARK HALL. THE GHOST OF HER VOICE, ITS ECHO, ITS REFLECTION. AN EMPTY HALL ALWAYS MAKES A VOICE SOUND BITTER AND METALLIC. THERE'S TOO MUCH REVERBERATION. THE CROWD THAT WILL SOON FILL THE HALL WILL ABSORB THE ECHO. IT WILL SOFTEN AND DAMPEN THE SOUND AND ADD ITS OWN SHOUTING, CHEERING, AND APPLAUSE. CÉLINE'S MIKE WILL CAPTURE IT ALL, AND SHE'LL HEAR THE NOISE OF THE CROWD ALONG WITH HER OWN VOICE.

*" And all that I am
And all that I'll be
Means nothing at all
If you can't be with me. "*

To do his job well, Patrick, René Angélil's oldest son, has to know the places where Céline performs like the back of his hand. And that includes monstrous arenas and amphitheaters. Early this morning, Patrick began to familiarize himself with the place: the passageways, the safety exits, the light and sound areas, the service sheds, the staircases, the corridors and hallways, the catwalks and walkways that run under the stands. He introduced himself to the security people who run messages and control the doors. He can move freely throughout the stadium and all its storage areas.

The voices of (from left to right) Julie LeBlanc, Terry Bradford, and Élise Duguay complement the beauty of Céline's songs. On tour, every evening they sing the same notes and words and repeat the same movements. Their routine might turn into sterile repetition if not for the physical pleasure they all get from using their voices and keeping them flexible and finely tuned.

Everyone in the crew and the entourage—nearly 100 people—wears a pass around their neck. A plastic badge with Céline's picture and the words "Falling into You Around the World" forming a halo around her head. This brightly colored card is the last of a series of passes, since the tour will be over in a few days. The design of the pass had to be changed several times so that it couldn't be counterfeited. Sometimes, when the crew would go out for a stroll before the show, they'd blend in with the crowds around the stadium and have to show their passes to get back in.

It was almost dark when Céline came to the concert hall. The stage set was perfectly familiar to her. It never changed from show to show. The boards of the stage, the steep ramp, the black curtain at the back, all the rest. In

"Plenty of things make me happy," Céline says. "But not good reviews or the cheers of the crowd. What I really love is when people come up to me and tell me that one of my songs has helped them face life, to kiss and make up, to feel good about themselves or even…to accept the inevitable. That's why I sing. Singing for me is reaching out to people."

Osaka, Nagoya, and Seoul it was the same. She could walk around that stage with her eyes closed. She could find the banister that leads to the hidden stairs. Halfway down, on the left, there would be a light. To the right, the plexiglass shield that protects Dominique Messier's drums. At the foot of the stairs to the left, attached to the banister will be a little shelf with a box of tissues and a bottle of water.

When Céline steps on the stage, stage manager Claude Plante gives her a mike. He stands close by during the entire performance, just out of sight, ready to help if help is needed. When she leaves the stage, his hand will reach out from the same place, at the same height, to lead her to the stairway.

For months on end, this has been the world Céline knows best, the most reassuring place in a constantly changing landscape. The dressing room varies

from one concert hall to the next, and she rarely sleeps more than three nights in the same bed. But since last winter, the stage has been the same, as have the people who work on it.

She greets her six musicians, three back-up singers, and all her technicians one at a time. She calls them "sweetheart," "my love," "honey." She asks after their sick mother or their pregnant wife. Céline Dion is direct and uncom-

A GIRL CAN DREAM, CAN'T SHE?

WHEN SHE WAS YOUNGER, CÉLINE DREAMED OF STANDING AT THE TOP OF A SPIRAL STAIRCASE, THEN SLOWLY, GRACEFULLY DESCENDING TOWARD THE FANS, SINGING THE MOST MOVING SONG THAT'S EVER BEEN SUNG.

WHEN SHE WAS DESIGNING THE OPENING OF THE "FALLING INTO YOU" SHOW, SHE REMEMBERED THAT DREAM. RENÉ ENCOURAGED HER TO FOLLOW THROUGH ON IT—"GO ALL OUT," HE SAID. IN PLACE OF A STAIRCASE, THEY USED A VERY STEEP RAMP. HALFWAY DOWN, ON THE LEFT, STANDS THE KIND OF LAMPPOST YOU SEE IN PARIS. THERE ARE SEATS FOR THE MUSICIANS ON EACH SIDE. SHE WOULD SING THE FIRST TWO COUPLETS OF THE SONG IN DARKNESS, A TOTAL OF ABOUT TWENTY SECONDS. WHEN SHE CAME TO THE CHORUS, "'CAUSE I'M YOUR LADY, AND YOU ARE MY MAN," SHE WOULD WALK INTO THE LIGHT.

plicated, easily approachable, concerned with others. That's her nature; that's the way she was brought up.

❝It does me good to kiss my friends and tell them I love them. It reassures me. I do it as much for myself as for them, I admit it.... It's part of my nature now. I love the people I work with. That's why we work together—because we love each other.❞

She also greets Yves Aucoin, known as Lapin, the lighting man. He uses light as the prime building material for creating her stage effect. Smoke produced by machines behind the stage captures the light. Lapin uses it the way a painter uses a canvas. He sketches and projects his colors on it, and creates all kinds of striking visual effects. Smoke is his art museum. Lapin contrasts form and color to make whirlpools and caves and spirals, and in the middle of everything is Céline. Sometimes he surrounds her with clouds and makes golden rain fall upon her. Other times he flashes lightning across her face. Céline never sees Lapin's work because she's part of it. On stage, she is at the very heart of his kaleidoscope.

In contrast, while the show is in progress, some 30 people are at work in the shadows, in the belly of the beast, which is the concert hall, each one busy with his or her job. The show can't go on without them. Tall, handsome Patrick Angélil remains calm while taking care of dozens of last-minute details. Walkie-

talkies keep crew members in ready contact. The technicians are prepared for sudden changes. And the caterers from Snakatak keep all of them, including Céline, well fed.

Tonight, Céline knows, the show is going to be magic. She can feel something in the air. You never know when it's going to happen. That's the beauty of the stage: The unexpected can always happen. There are some nights when the magic just rains down.

Opposite page: *Céline goes all out in giving an exuberant, exhausting two-hour performance during every one of her shows. She performs with pleasure and passion and mastery.* Above: *Céline's powerful voice, combined with her natural charisma on stage, never fails to charm the crowd. At the end of the show, the audience is left wanting more.*

The Prelude

TROPICAL HEAT IS ALWAYS GOOD FOR THE VOICE. AFTER THE FEBRUARY TOUR OF THE BIG CITIES IN ASIA WITH THEIR COLD, DUSTY WIND, EVERYONE WAS FEELING TIRED. BANDAR SERI BEGAWAN, THE CAPITAL OF BRUNEI, SEEMED LIKE A WARM, SWEETLY PERFUMED OASIS, A LOVELY MOMENT OF RELAXATION BEFORE THE HUSTLE AND BUSTLE OF THE GRAMMY AWARDS. CÉLINE HAD BEEN NOMINATED IN FOUR CATEGORIES: BEST SONG OF THE YEAR ("BECAUSE YOU LOVED ME"), BEST POP-ROCK ALBUM, BEST POP-ROCK SINGER (ALONG WITH SHAWN COLVIN, GLORIA ESTEFAN, TONI BRAXTON, AND JEWEL) AND BEST ALBUM *(FALLING INTO YOU)*.

BRUNEI IS A LITTLE COUNTRY IN THE NORTHERN PART OF THE ISLAND OF BORNEO, VERY GREEN AND, THANKS TO OIL, IMMENSELY RICH. THE CAPITAL, BANDAR SERI BEGAWAN, HAS FEWER THAN 100,000 PEOPLE. THERE ARE WHOLE VILLAGES BUILT ENTIRELY ON STILTS, CHARMING PLACES THE MUSICIANS DECIDED TO EXPLORE. IT PROMISED TO BE A RESTFUL STOP.

THE SULTAN OF BRUNEI IS REPUTED TO BE THE RICHEST MAN IN THE WORLD. HE OFFERED CÉLINE AND HER ENTOURAGE TWO ENORMOUS MANSIONS WHOSE OPULENT ARCHITECTURE SEEMED TO BE STRAIGHT OUT OF *GONE WITH THE WIND*. THE DWELLINGS CAME COMPLETE WITH MAGNIFICENT GARDENS FILLED WITH BIRDS WHOSE SONGS POURED IN THROUGH THE OPEN WINDOWS. BEYOND THE GROUNDS STOOD THE EXUBERANT, LUXURIOUS JUNGLE.

ONE AFTERNOON, ALONG WITH SUZANNE, ERIC, DAVE, BARRY, MANON, AND GILLES, CÉLINE TOURED THE PROPERTY IN A GOLF CART. THEY ENCOUNTERED A VARIETY OF CATS AND A MONKEY FAMILY, WITH WHOM THEY PLAYED. HER FRIENDS WERE VERY MUCH IMPRESSED BY THE BEAUTY OF THE SURROUNDINGS AND THE WEALTH OF THE SETTING, WITH ITS SWIMMING POOL, TENNIS COURTS, GYM, AND AUDITORIUM. CÉLINE WAS IN A SILENT TIME, SO SHE POINTED AND OPENED HER EYES WIDE WHENEVER SHE SAW SOMETHING NEW AND ASTONISHING.

LATER, ONE OF THE PRINCES DROVE THEM IN A CART TO SEE HIS CAR COLLECTION. THERE WERE BENTLEYS, FERRARIS, MACLARENS, ROLLS ROYCES, BUGATIS,

Céline is gracious and joyful in her acceptance speech at the 1997 Grammy Awards for Falling into You. *She read from notes she prepared beforehand so she wouldn't forget to thank anybody in the excitement of the moment.*

15 years old, were intimidated, despite the hefty diamonds that decorated their fingers and hair. The younger boy, who was no more than six years old, was a natural actor, and not at all reserved like his older sisters. He played "Here's the church, here's the steeple" with Céline for an audience of 20 charmed adults.

Then Céline told them how she'd lost her voice once on the stage of a big theater in Paris. The children listened with rapt attention. The little boy took her hand when she described how she'd cried backstage at the Zenith Theater because she'd lost her voice.

"Did you ever find it?" he asked.

"I had to look for a long time," Céline answered. "Luckily, the people in the theater helped out."

"Did they close all the windows and all the doors?"

"They did that too. Then they looked under their seats, in their pockets and their purses. They found little bits of my voice everywhere."

"Even in their own mouths?"

"Even in their own mouths and their ears. We put the pieces back together. Then everyone sang along with me."

The little prince knew that they'd left reality behind, and that they were in fantasy now. He wasn't fooled by the story, but he loved it just the same.

Everyone took pictures. Céline struck up a friendship with one of the sultan's wives. They talked and laughed together and held hands. Céline makes friends wherever she goes.

and Lamborghinis. Some were new models, and others were antiques, all lined up in perfect silence.

In the evening, Céline and her entourage made their way to the castle, where four of the sultan's children, two boys and two girls, awaited them. Out of politeness, but also because she wanted to talk to the children, Céline broke her silence. In the great hall filled with trophies and placques, she sat with her back to the giant bay window, which looked out on a lawn as big as a half-dozen football fields—the sultan's private polo grounds. The two girls, 12 and

That's one of her great talents. Without asking, she approaches people. She enters their lives and goes straight to their heart. She moves them and makes them laugh. And she loves them. She almost always makes the first move. That's probably her way of controlling her safety, and of sharing those thoughts and feelings that she wants to. She would never tell the sultan's family and friends that she's scared the show she'll be giving tomorrow night might not turn out right. Even if she did, they wouldn't believe her. They all know she's sung in the world's top concert halls, and won over the most demanding audiences.

The invitation to Brunei had been waiting for some time now. René loved the idea. "Do you realize," he told everyone who'd listen, "just how few people have ever been invited by the Sultan of Brunei?"

Céline was singing in Seoul, South Korea, on February 21, and at the Grammys in New York on February 26. The technicians wouldn't have time to set up the stage in Brunei for her February 23 appearance. "What does that matter?" the sultan's representatives had asked Barry Garber. "We'll build an exact replica of the stage. The same dimensions, with all the equipment. We'll have the screens, the cameras, the consoles. Everything."

"Céline has to rest," René said. The sultan's people offered a positively attractive deal. "I'd never dare ask that much," he admitted, "not even for a giant sta-

At the press conference following the show, Céline proudly holds up her Grammy for Best Pop Album, awarded for Falling into You *at the 39th Annual Grammy Awards ceremony in New York on February 26, 1997.*

dium." But he still wasn't sure. Finally, the sultan's representatives promised that a private DC-8 would pick up Céline and her entourage in Seoul, take them to Brunei, then on to New York immediately after their show, in time for the Grammys.

All for an audience of 300. That's what's bothering Céline tonight. Her show is designed for big concert halls. She's not used to nightclubs or cabarets where the audience eats, drinks, and talks during the performance. And she's never enjoyed singing for captive audiences.

❝ *I always get the feeling I'm disturbing people. Everyone is talking, living their lives together, laughing and having fun. Then I show up with my big speakers and my lights. Maybe they don't particularly want to listen to me. Maybe they have a lot more important things to say to each other.* ❞

It may be a good omen. When Céline is worried, when she's tired, or in a bad mood, she gives her best. She works twice as hard. Ten times as hard.

Vocal Gymnastics

ÉLINE WARMS UP HER VOICE. FOR THE LAST FIVE YEARS, SHE HASN'T GONE ONSTAGE WITHOUT DOING HER WARM-UP AND STRETCHING EXERCISES FOR A GOOD HALF HOUR. HER TRAINER, DR. RILEY, CONVINCED HER TO ADOPT THE ROUTINE.

HER EXERCISES AREN'T THAT MUCH DIFFERENT FROM WHAT ATHLETES DO BEFORE A BIG GAME. SHE WORKS ON BREATHING AND STRETCHING, BENDING AND MASSAGING, UNTIL HER ENTIRE SYSTEM RELAXES. THEN HER VOCAL CORDS GET INVOLVED AND SHE PRODUCES PURE SOUND WITHOUT CONCERN FOR NOTES OR WORDS. HER VOICE SEEMS TO WANDER THROUGH THE SCALES. IT WILL FALL SILENT, STRIKE UP AGAIN, THEN SHE'LL GRAB A NOTE AND HOLD IT FOR WHAT SEEMS LIKE AN ETERNITY. SHE'LL PLACE HER FINGERS ON HER NOSE TO FEEL THE VIBRATION. HER VOICE SLIPS SLOWLY INTO HER THROAT, STILL HOLDING THAT SAME NOTE LIKE A BIRD OF PREY. IT REACHES HER BELLY, DEEP INSIDE HER, THEN EMERGES SLOWLY AND POURS FROM HER MOUTH LIKE THE FLIGHT OF DOVES.

THE SECOND OF CÉLINE'S VOCAL EXERCISES BARELY INVOLVES HER VOCAL CORDS AT ALL. SHE KEEPS HER VOICE IN HER MOUTH, RIGHT ON HER LIPS. THAT TECHNIQUE PRODUCES A VIBRATING SOUND, SIMILAR TO THE KIND OF NOISE PEOPLE MAKE WHEN THEY'RE COLD, OR WHEN A CHILD WANTS TO IMITATE A CAR OR AN AIRPLANE.

"THAT EXERCISE TELLS ME WHAT STATE MY VOICE IS IN. AND THE STATE OF MY NERVES AND MY VOICE, TOO. BECAUSE IT TAKES A LOT OF CONTROL. IF I'M NOT IN GOOD SHAPE, I'LL FIND OUT RIGHT AWAY. IT'S A LITTLE LIKE AN X RAY."

THE LITTLE PLANE BUZZES THROUGH THE WINDOWLESS ROOM, A KIND OF BUNKER WITH CONCRETE BLOCK WALLS. THEN IT FADES INTO THE DISTANCE. CÉLINE IS WEARING A PAIR OF BLACK LEATHER PANTS AND A TIGHT BLACK SWEATER. SHE WALKS THROUGH HER DRESSING ROOM WITH HER ARMS CROSSED AND TAKES A SIP OF WARM, HONEYED WATER.

Above: *Julie Leblanc (left) joined Céline's chorus of back-up singers during the "Falling into You" tour in Memphis.* Opposite page: *When Céline steps onstage, she is completely in character; totally in control. Her only goal is to make sure she gives the audience what they came for: a good time.*

66 *Some days, my voice is dull. It doesn't want to listen to me or answer when I call it. It tries to get away from me. When that happens, I go into a room with it and lock the door, whether I'm at the hotel or in my dressing room. I talk to my voice, I struggle with it, I care for it, I caress it, and in the end, it always listens to me.* 99

As the tour progresses, Céline and her singers put their voices to work ever harder. They sing even when they're not onstage. Without even realizing it, their exercise sessions grow a little longer every day.

66 *My voice has a memory of its own. When I'm on tour and singing the same songs, I force a lot less. I sing without thinking, and I never need to remind myself to hit one note harder than another.* 99

The third vocal exercise is a group one. Today, Céline and her back-up singers will make an inventory of all the different textures that their voices can produce. They move quickly from crystal to sandpaper, they get rough and gritty, then they turn smooth and sound like a caress, and break off again with the suddenness of a gunshot.

To finish up, they'll pant and sing the sounds "eeee" and "ahhh" and "oou" as high as they can, high enough to shatter glass, hitting each note hard, then quickly changing their rhythm and tone.

There's no way to describe that whirlpool of sound. Their voices mingle. Elise reaches high into the scale, Rachelle is bluesy and sultry, Céline is supple and powerful.

To keep from straining her voice, she has to stay in superb shape. Holding back can take a lot of energy. Mastering her voice demands concentration. When Céline gets tired, you can feel the effort. The musicians and sound people pay complete attention to her voice during every performance. They can sense the pain and fear and fatigue. A veil, or an imperfection, or a scratch can sometimes appear on the highest notes. The effect is beautiful and very sensual. And disturbing too. It's as though her voice could break at any minute.

In the Dressing Room

RIGHT AFTER THE SOUND CHECK, LOULOU ESCORTS CÉLINE INTO HER DRESSING ROOM. SHE HAS SET OUT LARGE BOUQUETS OF FRESHLY CUT FLOWERS AND HAS PLUGGED IN HUMIDIFIERS AND SPACE HEATERS. ALL ARTISTS LIKE A WARM DRESSING ROOM. LOULOU OPENS UP THE PORTABLE WARDROBE AND THE CLOSET WHERE THE COSTUMES ARE HUNG. SHE SETS UP THE MAKEUP TABLE WITH ITS BRIGHTLY LIT MIRROR. SHE OPENS THE VIALS OF FACE CREAM AND PLACES THEM ON THE TABLE, ALONG WITH THICK WHITE TOWELS, POWDER, EYELINER, BRUSHES, AND LIPSTICK. HERE AND THERE, SHE SCATTERS CÉLINE'S GOOD-LUCK CHARMS: STUFFED FROGS AND AMULETS.

CÉLINE AND HER CREW ARE LIKE NOMADS WHO PITCH THEIR TENT IN A DIFFERENT SPOT EVERY NIGHT, BUT WHO ALWAYS FIND WHAT THEY NEED TO MAKE THEM FEEL AT HOME. THE DRESSING ROOM IS HER PRIVATE COCOON WHERE A CATERPILLAR BECOMES A BUTTERFLY, WHERE THE SINGER WILL BECOME A STAR. ALL ALONE, SHE'LL PUT ON THE COSTUME THAT HELPS HER FACE THE WORLD, AND CONCENTRATE ALL HER ENERGY BEFORE STEPPING OUT ONTO THE STAGE.

SEEING A STAR IN HER DRESSING ROOM IS LIKE SURPRISING AN EXOTIC BIRD IN ITS NEST. IN BIG CITIES, GOING BACKSTAGE IS A MUCH COVETED HONOR. IN PARIS, LONDON, OR NEW YORK, THERE'S ALWAYS SOMEONE WHO INSISTS HE'S A VIP, AND WHO SHOWS UP AT THE DRESSING ROOM DOOR, WANTING TO SEE CÉLINE. ERIC SHIFTS HIS WEIGHT FROM ONE FOOT TO THE OTHER, KEEPING AN EYE ON THE SELF-PROCLAIMED VIP, THEN TELLS HIM THAT CÉLINE IS BUSY.

THIS EVENING AT WEMBLEY, THE DRESSING ROOM DOOR WAS WIDE OPEN, AND ERIC STOOD A BIT TO ONE SIDE TO LET IN THE FRESH AIR. BY NOW, THE SHOW IS A WELL-OILED MACHINE. THERE'S LESS STRESS AND LESS STAGE FRIGHT. BUT THE DRESSING ROOM WAS OVERFLOWING. A RETIRED MAGICIAN CAME IN AND STARTED PASSING OUT BUSINESS CARDS. HE REMINISCED WITH RENÉ ABOUT MONTREAL NIGHTLIFE IN THE 1940S AND 1950S. RENÉ LISTENED TO HIM POLITELY.

THEN CAME A VOICE—LOUD AND STRONG. IT BELONGED TO FRENCH STAGE AND SCREEN STAR GÉRARD DEPARDIEU. HE SWEPT INTO THE DRESSING ROOM AND

Céline's dressing room is her private sanctuary; her sister Manon is her trusted and beloved confidante. Manon remains at her side wherever she goes, helping her out, supporting her, and taking care of her.

immediately took center stage. Céline just melts every time she hears the music of Depardieu's voice. In Paris, Depardieu came into Céline's dressing room after her show. The place was packed with writers, fashion people, movie stars. Céline was a prisoner in her own crowded dressing room. Then Depardieu strode up to her and took her face between his hands as if they were old friends, with no one else around.

Céline is a true singer. That's what Gérard Depardieu told her in her Wembley dressing room, a few minutes before she stepped on stage in front of 15,000 people who were stamping their feet and calling her name. He talked about the show he'd attended at the Bercy concert hall, outside Paris. "Your voice fascinated me. It goes right to the heart, I'm telling you." He took her head in his hands again. "You sing with your soul. You know, some people study for years and years in conservatories and theater schools to reach that point—to

make their soul visible, just a little piece of their soul—but they don't make it happen the way you do. Your soul is visible, your whole soul, and that's your beauty."

Céline likes to have guests before the show. That way, she knows it won't go on too long. After the show, she'd rather be alone with her friends.

❝*I put on two shows. One on stage and one in the dressing room. It's pure bliss on stage. In my dressing room, I have to make an extra effort. I feel like I'm empty sometimes. It's true, I could keep my mouth closed and think my own thoughts, but I just can't. People come up to me, often they're intimidated, and I help them. I can't stop myself. I don't know how to be any other way: I want to please people. I reach out to them. Sometimes I wonder why. Some of them aren't even very nice. But I want them to love me. I smile and make them laugh. That's part of my job, and I do it the best way I know how.*❞

It was five minutes before 9:00 when René came and told Depardieu kindly but firmly that it was time for him to leave. Céline had to face the solitude of the stage on her own.

When it's time to step out on the stage, most artists suffer from stage fright. Sometimes it can be hell. They forget where they are and what they're supposed to be doing. They think of the show they're about to begin and realize they can't remember anything: the song order, the words, the names of their band members. They'll be booed off stage.

Céline generally keeps her cool. A few days ago, five minutes before going on, she videotaped a thank-you message for the people at 550 Music, the American branch of Sony for whom she records. She was sitting at her makeup table, her hair all done, her makeup on, in the outfit she wears to perform. She looked straight into the camera and told the promotion people at 550 that she owed her success in the United States to them. "I'm singing here at Wembley tonight, and it's all because of the work you've done," she said. They were all a big family, and she was proud to be a part of it. She wished them a happy and healthy new year. She blew them a kiss. It was perfect. Exactly one and a half minutes. One take.

She thanked the cameraman and the soundman, then went to her mirror. The cameraman and the soundman didn't move. Céline caught their anxious look and turned to René. "There isn't anything else, is there?" she asked.

Of course there was something else. She had to improvise another 60-second spot for the annual meeting of the presidents of her American fan clubs. She meditated for a minute, more to get back into the mood than to find the right words, because improvising is no problem with her. Then she gave warm thanks to her American fan clubs as the cameras whirred. Everyone applauded in the dressing room. But she wasn't happy.

"I just know they'll see I did it at the last minute. It's like I was just getting it out of the way, don't you think?"

Everyone contradicted her. Then René herded them out of the room. The show was set to start in five minutes. It was on to the next thing.

Most artists experience some form of stage fright before a big show. Céline is no different: Although she thrives on the stress and excitement her performances bring on, she still has to cross that river of darkness by herself, the one that separates her from the brightly lit stage. Her friends will move aside, one by one. She'll summon the stage fright and it will fill her mind, and she will confront it straight on before facing the crowd.

Backstage Games

THE IMPATIENT CROWD IS PUTTING ON A LITTLE SHOW OF ITS OWN, DOING THE WAVE. YOU CAN HEAR THEM SHOUTING AND CHANTING ALL THE WAY BACK TO THE DRESSING ROOM AND THE OFFICES. CÉLINE LOVES HEARING THE CROWDS. EVERY ONE HAS ITS OWN VOICE, ITS OWN RHYTHM, ITS OWN TONE. JAPANESE CROWDS, ESPECIALLY IN TOKYO, ARE SO WELL BEHAVED THAT ONCE CÉLINE ASKED MICHEL TO GO SNEAK A PEEK INSIDE THE BUDOKAN HALL TO SEE IF THERE WAS ANYONE THERE. IN NÎMES OR NUREMBERG OR MARSEILLE, EVERYWHERE IN EUROPE, THE CROWDS ARE COMPLETELY DIFFERENT. THEY CHANT HER NAME AND SEEM SO IMPATIENT THAT SHE WONDERS WHETHER THEY'RE GOING TO TEAR THE PLACE APART.

BE THEY WELL BEHAVED OR WILD, YOU SHOULD NEVER KEEP A CROWD WAITING. FIFTEEN MINUTES BEFORE SHOW TIME, THERE WILL BE NO ONE AROUND CÉLINE BUT HER TRUSTED FRIENDS. MANON AND LOULOU AND ERIC, AND SOMETIMES MICHEL AND SUZANNE.

USING FLUORESCENT TAPE, THE TECHNICIANS HAVE TRACED A PATH AMONG THE MACHINERY AND THE COILS OF WIRE AND CABLE. IN THE DARKNESS, YOU CAN SEE THE LUMINOUS COMPUTER SCREENS. JUST BEFORE SHE CROSSES INTO THAT ZONE OF DARKNESS, CÉLINE STOPS AND TURNS BACK TOWARD LOULOU AND MANON. SHE'S WEARING A LONG, HOODED CAPE THAT COVERS HER THROAT. LOULOU HOLDS OUT A CRACKER AND A GLASS OF WARM WATER. THE CRACKER CLEANS HER THROAT AND VOCAL CORDS, AND THE WARM WATER HELPS THE CRACKER GO DOWN. MANON PUSHES BACK THE HOOD AND FIXES A FEW STRANDS OF HER HAIR.

THERE HAVE BEEN TIMES—IN OTHER CITIES—WHEN, JUST BEFORE STEPPING OUT FROM BEHIND THE CURTAIN, CÉLINE'S STAGE FRIGHT HAS ESCALATED.

IN WALES, SHE LOOKED AT HER BROTHER MICHEL AND ASKED, ALMOST IN A PANIC, "WHERE ARE WE?"

"CARDIFF," MICHEL REASSURED HER.

"CARDIFF?"

"WITH TWO F'S."

Céline and her band have a rapport that enables them to lift the music to emotional peaks, drawing the audience into the magic of the show.

"Two f's? What difference does that make?"

They laughed. She still had cracker crumbs in her mouth. She blew them out. They laughed some more. In the minute or two before going on stage, she has a visceral need to laugh. Michel is used to it.

As she prepares to go on stage tonight, she's still nervous. Milan's Forum doesn't hold more than 8,000 people. But this is Céline's first contact with the city, and first meetings can be stressful. Only laughter can dissipate fear and stage fright. Michel fools around to help his sister relax. He found an old broom in one of the corridors, and now he's pretending to sweep the floor in front of Céline, like a curling player, while she

bends down and acts as though she's sliding the stone down the surface.

A giant cheer goes up in the Forum. The house lights have just been turned off. Stage manager Claude Plante takes Céline by the hand and leads her along the narrow pathway studded with arrows of fluorescent tape, all the way to the steep stairs that she'll climb alone.

She stands very straight at the back of the stage, inside the protective cocoon formed by the curtains. In the shadows, the musicians turn to look her way. It's her last moment alone.

Many artists, professional athletes, and politicians who perform before large crowds do things for luck. Céline loves ritual. She has a large number of superstitions and private ceremonies. Her lucky number is five, which came to her early in her career. For years, every time she saw a nickel on the ground, she'd bend down and pick it up.

In a little clear plastic envelope at the bottom of her purse, she carries a coin she found on a stage in Trois-Rivières, in Quebec. As she always does after her first two songs, she talked to the crowd that night, thanking them for coming, telling them how much she loved them, and how she hoped they'd have a good time. Suddenly, she spotted a shiny coin with a beaver on it, tail-side up, right at the edge of the stage. Réne once told her never to pick up a coin if it was tail-side up. "If it's tails, let it lie. It'll bring bad luck." But at intermission in Trois-Rivières, after the curtain fell, she leaned over and turned the coin so the head side showed, then picked it up. It's been her good-luck charm ever since.

During the "Incognito" tour, before the curtain rose, she would perform a complex ritual, a kind of childish game that was both serious and reassuring. The ritual has changed over time, but it's still as necessary as ever. It's not a game. For Céline, every movement has magical powers. She needs them, especially when she's on tour, far from her familiar surroundings, when every night the dressing room, the hotel, the concert hall, and the crowds are different. These little games give her a sense of stability, familiarity, and intimacy.

Before René leaves backstage to slip into the concert hall, two or three minutes before she crosses the river of shadow that separates her from the light, she walks up to him. He holds out his left hand, palm open like an offering. She takes his palm and places the fingers of her right hand in it. Then with her other hand, she closes René's hand over her fingers. The ritual means everything to her because of its symbolism. René's palm is the bowl, the cradle, the vessel, the nest. She places her hand, her life, her future in it.

Then, everyone who's part of the show—the musicians, back-up singers, and the dozens of technicians—will participate in the right thumb ceremony. In the seconds before the curtain goes up, Céline will turn to each of her musicians and singers, look them in the eye, and

As she does before every show, Céline participates in a reassuring ritual, exchanging thumbs-up signs with the musicians and back-up singers. These little games give her a sense of stability, familiarity, and intimacy when she's on tour, far from familiar surroundings.

throw out her arms, thumbs up. They smile and raise their thumbs too. Then she'll go through the same ritual with Daniel Baron on her right, Jeff and Loulou at the foot of the stairway behind her, then her brother Michel, her sister Manon, and Suzanne.

In Birmingham one night, Michel got caught in the curtains and couldn't find the way out. His panicked sisters went looking for him in the darkness. Finally, he had to slip under the curtain and run to the foot of the stairway to raise his thumbs in his sister's direction. Only then did the stage manager give the signal. Lapin threw the stage into darkness, and a strong wind began to blow.

And Céline stepped on stage, totally in control. A strong woman with strong feelings, a star, completely herself.

The Show

AT FIRST YOU HEAR THE WORDS, BARELY AUDIBLE, SCATTERED BY THE WIND THROUGH THE DARK, ELECTRIC AIR, HIGH ABOVE THE CORAL SKY AMPHITHEATER. THE MURMUR OF THE CROWD CRACKLES WITH ANTICIPATION. YOU CAN CATCH A FEW PHRASES, THE WORD *LOVE* NO DOUBT, A WHISPERED *I LOVE YOU*, SOFT BUT STRONG. THEN, SUDDENLY, A VOICE RISES FROM THE CHAOS, CLEAR AND TRUE. THE CROWD AND THE WIND FALL SILENT, AND EVERY HEART IS CAPTURED:

> "THE WHISPERS IN THE MORNING
> OF LOVERS SLEEPING TIGHT
> ARE ROLLING LIKE THUNDER NOW
> AS I LOOK IN YOUR EYES."

LIGHTNING FLASHES, ERRATIC LIGHT FLYING OUT OF CONTROL, SPLITTING THE DARKNESS AND THROWING FURTIVE SHADOWS ACROSS THE CLOUDS OF SMOKE RISING FROM THE STAGE. THE CROWD SEARCHES TO FIND THE SPOT THE VOICE IS COMING FROM. FINALLY THEY SEE CÉLINE AT THE TOP OF THE RUNWAY THAT CUTS THE STAGE IN TWO.

> "I HOLD ON TO YOUR BODY
> AND FEEL EACH MOVE YOU MAKE
> YOUR VOICE IS WARM AND TENDER
> A LOVE THAT I COULD NOT FORSAKE."

"THE POWER OF LOVE" IS AN EROTIC SONG, THE STORY OF A TORRID LOVE SCENE. THE 20 SONGS THAT MAKE UP THE "FALLING INTO YOU" SHOW ALL SPEAK OF LOVE—SIMPLE, CLASSIC, ETERNAL LOVE BETWEEN A MAN AND A WOMAN.

JUST AS CÉLINE LAUNCHES INTO THE CHORUS, THE STAGE IS BATHED IN BRIGHT LIGHT, AND HER FACE APPEARS ON THE GIANT SCREENS ON EITHER SIDE OF THE STAGE. THE CROWD LEAPS TO ITS FEET. FOR THE REST OF THE SHOW, CÉLINE WILL BE ENVELOPED IN LIGHT, EXPOSED TO EVERY EYE, SINGING OF LOVE.

" Cause I'm your lady
And you are my man
Whenever you reach for me
I'll do all that I can . . . . "

Céline ends the song. She lets the applause wash over her, then tells the people, "I feel so wonderful being home with you tonight." Her voice is like velvet. Her words and the texture of her voice are sexy, soothing. The Coral Sky Amphitheater goes crazy. The current rushes between Céline and the crowd. The show is going to be pure pleasure.

During a show a perfect union among the band members is bound to happen sooner or later. Most of the time, it's a subjective thing. Mégo, Picard, and Messier may be delighted and think *what a great show,* while Céline, Frulla, and Langis aren't completely pleased. Or the other way around. There are shows that start off slow and wind up with a roar. Once in a blue moon, there's absolute consensus, epiphany, total magic. Everything clicks from beginning to end. That's when Céline and her musicians look each other in the eye and smile blissfully. They're happy, each in his own world, yet together. In the end there will be consensus on which were the unforgettable shows of the "Falling into You" tour.

There's always a danger. When an audience is conquered too soon, it can feel disappointed or neglected. When a crowd starts off cold, like they did one night in Buffalo, Céline mobilizes all her energy, intelligence, and charm to seduce them. She'll do whatever she has to do. She'll work her voice harder, she'll heighten the emotion. And when the audience rises to its feet, when the people have been conquered, when they give her an ovation, only then will she savor sweet victory. But tonight there's no need to dig deep into her energy reserve. The Coral Sky gets to its feet again when she sings "River Deep, Mountain High." She rides their ovations with natural grace.

Céline accepts her award for Best Female Vocalist at the 1996 World Music Awards while presenters Bo Derek and Tony Bennett look on.

"I see a lot of my neighbors tonight," she says, smiling.

Bryon Rivers, a writer with the *Palm Beach Post,* scribbles in his notebook, "Dion doesn't have stage presence; she *is* stage presence."

It's been said many times: Céline's presence is her greatest asset. She knows how to hold the stage and communicate with her audience. And her communication is always true, simple, and filled with infinite warmth.

She's been touring almost constantly for two years. She's seen Canada, the United States, Europe, the Pacific Rim, Asia. At the end of March 1996, she and her team decided to shake up the show a little. They changed the songs, costumes, and sets. Some of the songs from the old show had become a little tired. Others, from the *Falling into You* album, needed to be featured. With an eye to promoting the album, Céline and René gave the whole show a makeover. She asked for a month to rehearse the new version.

But she got so busy with promotion, making videos, and television appearances that Mégo, the band leader, started to worry. René promised him a week of rehearsals, which rapidly dwindled to four days, then two. Mégo rehearsed with the musicians, but without Céline. They were ready; they knew the music and were in control of their part of the show. He was confident that Céline would learn fast. But Lapin was worried. He had designed his lighting and chosen color motifs for every song.

"When I'm onstage," Céline says, "everything seems so unreal to me. I'm in control, of course. I have absolute control. It makes my head spin. I know what I'm doing at every second, the way a racecar driver feels. But just like the driver, I have no time to take in the scenery. Everything's happening too fast."

But since he didn't know how Céline would move on the stage, he couldn't place the spotlights. In the end, they were able to squeeze in only three hours of rehearsal in the old Montreal Forum. In three hours, they made a quick inventory of the worst mistakes, but there was no time to correct them, except in each performer's mind. Everybody was terribly nervous.

The new show premiered in Vancouver on May 18, 1996. Things got off to a rough start. Everyone was so busy trying not to make a mistake that there was no harmony between the parts. The critics hammered away, but no one failed to mention Céline's powerful voice, the quality of her stage presence, how effortlessly she could charm the audience, how spontaneous and direct and natural she was. And no one failed to mention that the audience begged for more.

Her Song

AS CÉLINE SINGS "SEDUCES ME" THE FANS COME AND LAY OFFERINGS AT HER FEET. EVERYTHING FROM STUFFED FROGS AND TEDDY BEARS TO FLOWERS, NICKELS, CAKES, COOKIES, FRUITS, JARS OF JAM, AND LETTERS. AFTER THEY'VE LEFT THEIR OFFERINGS AT THE EDGE OF THE STAGE, MOST OF THE FANS HURRY BACK TO THEIR SEATS, BUT SOME STAY RIGHT AT CÉLINE'S FEET WITH HEADS HIGH, OFTEN WITH ARMS EXTENDED. THEY'RE WAITING FOR HER TO LOOK THEIR WAY, TO TOUCH THEM. SOMETIMES SHE DOES. SHE BENDS OVER AND TOUCHES THEIR FINGERTIPS. OFTEN THEY'RE LITTLE GIRLS HELD UP BY THEIR PARENTS. CÉLINE CALLS THEM "CUTIE-PIE" OR "SWEETHEART."

SHE ALWAYS INTRODUCES "SEDUCES ME" AS ONE OF HER FAVORITE SONGS. IT'S LIKE A QUIET GARDEN AFTER THE THUNDERING WHIRLPOOL OF "RIVER DEEP, MOUNTAIN HIGH." IN A FEW SECONDS, WITH A FEW NOTES PLUCKED BY ANDRÉ COUTU ON HIS UNACCOMPANIED GUITAR, THE HALL PLUNGES INTO A COMPLETELY DIFFERENT ATMOSPHERE. IT'S THE MAGIC OF MUSIC, WITH ALL ITS EXTRAORDINARY PULL ON OUR EMOTIONS. CÉLINE CHANGES HER VOICE LIKE SHE CHANGES HER GOWNS. LIKE A PAINTER CHANGES PIGMENTS OR BRUSHES. SHE BRINGS OUT HER BLUESY VOICE, HER PALE, SOFT VOICE THAT CONTRASTS SO STRONGLY WITH THE DARK, HARD, BRASSY, CUTTING VOICE SHE USES WHEN SHE SINGS THE BIG, POWERFUL BALLADS LIKE "RIVER DEEP, MOUNTAIN HIGH" OR "THE POWER OF LOVE." THE CROWD SUBSIDES.

SHE ALWAYS FINISHES "SEDUCES ME" SITTING DOWN, IN FRONT OF THE BACK-UP SINGERS, AT THE FOOT OF THE LAMPPOST, DRAWN IN AND WRAPPED UP IN EMOTION. AS THE APPLAUSE SWELLS SHE KEEPS HER HEAD DOWN, HER HANDS FOLDED. THEN, ON THE GUITAR'S FINAL NOTES, SHE STANDS UP AND STRIDES TOWARD THE AUDIENCE. IN CHICAGO, SHE KNELT AT THE EDGE OF THE STAGE AND PLANTED A KISS ON THE CHEEK OF A LITTLE GIRL WHOSE MOTHER HAD PERCHED HER THERE. WHEN CÉLINE GOT TO HER FEET, MÉGO SWUNG INTO THE FIRST CHORDS OF "ALL BY MYSELF" AND THE CROWD THAT SEEMED HYPNOTIZED BY

Near right: *Céline and renowned international record producer David Foster mug for the camera at a benefit for AIDS research at Carnegie Hall. When Foster first heard Céline sing, he was bowled over by her voice and was convinced immediately that she had what it takes to make it big.* Opposite page: *For most people, dreams and real life are two separate worlds. For Céline Dion, those two worlds have become one. She's worked long and hard to make her dreams come true, but now her star shines as brightly as anyone could ever have dared to imagine.*

"Seduces Me" quickly shook itself awake.

What makes a song like "All By Myself" so touching? Of course, there's Céline's skill as a vocalist. David Foster rearranged the melody to make the most of her voice. But the song itself also tells a heartrending, emotional story, which is brought to life by the power of Céline's voice and the depth of feeling she puts into her performance.

During the musical transition (with Mégo's face featured in close-up on the big screens) Céline walks back up the ramp toward center stage. Legs braced, she belts out the last refrain, straight to the heart. It's the show's highest note, and she holds it until the audience is on its feet.

WHEN A SONG FADES

THE SONG CÉLINE HAS PERFORMED MOST OFTEN IN HER SHOWS IS "WHERE DOES MY HEART BEAT NOW." RECORDED IN LONDON IN MARCH 1989, IT WAS HER FIRST SONG TO HIT THE *BILLBOARD* CHARTS, AND EVER SINCE THEN IT HAS BEEN FEATURED IN ALMOST EVERY ONE OF HER SHOWS.

"IT'S A MAGNIFICENT SONG; I REALLY LIKE IT. BUT SOME NIGHTS SINGING THE SAME WORDS IS LIKE DOING HARD LABOR. THE HARD THING ISN'T TO SING THE SONG, TO CONTROL MY BREATHING, TO PUSH THE NOTES, BUT TO PUT MY HEART AND SOUL INTO IT. SOME NIGHTS I FEEL DISTRAUGHT; MY HEART FEELS COLD. I GET ENERGY BY GENERATING THE HEAT IT TAKES TO REALLY GET INTO EACH OF MY SONGS, EVEN THE ONES I'VE SUNG 100 OR 300 TIMES.

"I'M FORTUNATE TO HAVE A HUGE REPERTOIRE, DOZENS OF SONGWRITERS AND COMPOSERS WHO WORK FOR ME. WHICH MEANS I CAN CHANGE MY SHOWS REGULARLY. BUT AT THE SAME TIME, I HAVE TO GIVE PEOPLE WHAT THEY WANT. AND PEOPLE STILL WANT 'WHERE DOES MY HEART BEAT NOW' SEVERAL YEARS LATER.

"WITH ANY SONG, THERE'S ALWAYS A HONEYMOON. I DISCOVER IT, AND SOMETIMES IT'S LOVE AT FIRST SIGHT (AS WITH 'CALLING YOU'). THEN, ONE FINE DAY, I REALIZE THE MAGIC IS GONE.

"IN TORONTO [ON JUNE 23, 1996], I FELT LIKE I WAS COMPLETELY OUTSIDE THE SONG. NO MATTER HOW MUCH I TOLD MYSELF THAT I LIKED IT, NO MATTER THAT IT HAD BEEN MY FAITHFUL COMPANION FOR ALL THESE YEARS, I JUST COULDN'T GET INTO IT. I JUST HELD MY BREATH AND DOVE INTO A PIECE OF MUSIC THAT SUDDENLY SEEMED DARK AND MURKY.

"THEN, ALL OF A SUDDEN, IT OCCURRED TO ME THAT THE SONG DESCRIBED EXACTLY WHAT I WAS GOING THROUGH. WHERE DOES MY OWN HEART BEAT NOW? FOR WHOM? WHY? WHERE IS MY VOICE, MY BREATH?

"THAT'S HOW I GOT BACK INTO THE SONG. THAT'S HOW I FELL IN LOVE WITH IT ALL OVER AGAIN."

"I FEEL MY HEART BEAT NOW
NOW THAT I'VE FOUND
THE FEELING LIVES INSIDE."

The Monologue

THE MORE THAN TWO MILLION PEOPLE IN THE AMERICAS, EUROPE, AND ASIA WHO SAW CÉLINE DION'S 1996–97 TOUR MUST HAVE GOTTEN A PRETTY GOOD IDEA OF WHO SHE IS, WHERE SHE COMES FROM, AND THE LIFE SHE LIVES. THEY LEARNED INTIMATE DETAILS ABOUT HER LIFE JUST BY LISTENING TO HER TALK ON THE STAGE. THE THINGS CÉLINE SAYS IN HER SHOWS GIVE PEOPLE A CLOSE-UP, PERSONAL INSIGHT INTO HER CHARACTER, INTO THE WAY SHE FEELS ABOUT SHOW BUSINESS. HER MONOLOGUES ARE LITTLE GEMS OF CHARM AND PERSUASION.

AFTER "ALL BY MYSELF," SHE ASKS MÉGO, THE BANDLEADER, TO WAIT A FEW MINUTES. "I WANT TO TALK," SHE SAYS. THEN, TURNING TO THE CROWD THAT PACKS THE ENTERTAINMENT CENTER IN PERTH, AUSTRALIA, AT THE FAR END OF THE WORLD, SHE ADDS, "YOU ALL KNOW HOW I LOVE TO SING. BUT DID YOU KNOW I LOVE TO TALK, TOO?"

AND THE CROWD, REALIZING THAT SHE'S GOING TO TAKE THEM INTO HER CONFIDENCE, IS HAPPY. IN LESS THAN FIVE MINUTES CÉLINE WILL HAVE DRAWN HER OWN SELF-PORTRAIT, A LITTLE MASTERPIECE OF BREVITY, AND A STOREHOUSE OF INFORMATION ABOUT HERSELF TOUCHING ON THE SUBJECTS THAT PUT PEOPLE AT EASE: FAMILY, CHILDHOOD, SCHOOL DAYS.

SHE SPEAKS IN QUESTIONS, AND IT ISN'T LONG BEFORE THE CROWD IS ON HER SIDE.

"DID YOU KNOW I GREW UP SPEAKING FRENCH?"

THERE ARE SHOUTS OF RESPONSE FROM HERE AND THERE IN THE ENTERTAINMENT CENTER.

"MAYBE YOU DIDN'T KNOW THAT I'M THE YOUNGEST OF 14 CHILDREN."

THE AUDIENCE SHOUTS, LOUDER STILL. THEY KNOW ALL THAT. CÉLINE PRETENDS TO BE DISCOURAGED. "YOU KNOW EVERYTHING. I'M WASTING MY TIME."

THEN, IN A TRUSTING TONE, SHE ADDS, "WHEN THERE WERE 16 OF US AT THE DINNER TABLE, WE HAD TO KEEP OUR MOUTHS SHUT. SO TODAY, WHENEVER I GET THE CHANCE, I TALK!"

Céline's song, "Let's Talk About Love," debuted on a special episode of Sesame Street *in 1997.*

She tells how her parents didn't want children when they married. "Poor dad!" And her face, in close-up, has a disappointed look. Then, shaking her head, she says, "I mean, poor mom!" And with her hand she sketches a pregnant belly.

She recalls how she began singing when she was little, how her brothers and sisters stood her up on top of the kitchen table and stuck crayons in her hands.

In a stage whisper, she says, "I knew it wasn't a microphone. I'm not crazy, you know."

Then she goes back to her starting point. She tells the crowd that she was all the rage in her native Quebec long before she could speak English. And that she was always fascinated by American culture, by songs, movies, and TV shows made in the United States.

"Have you seen *Flashdance*? You remember the scene where the girl dances in the shower? Remember the song 'What a Feeling'? I was twelve years old when I had my first real show, with music, lighting, my own production crew. That's the song I sang."

After a pause she adds, "Well, believe it or not, I didn't understand a single word I was singing."

And the crowd bursts into laughter.

Throughout the tour, and not only in Perth, Céline introduces herself as the girl from far away, from a different culture, from a place that's not exactly American.

Then she explains how she took English lessons. From 9:00 A.M. until 5:00 P.M., five days a week. It was long, hard, and marvelous. "What a pleasure it is to learn," she exclaims.

After that, it's on to teachers. "I love teachers," she tells the people of Perth, which never fails to produce shouts, laughter, and good-humored booing. "Are there any teachers in the audience?" A few raise their hands timidly. Céline tells them she likes them because they're perfectionists. "Real teachers want to teach us something, and they want us to learn it well.

"We French-speakers have a hard time making some of the sounds that are common in English. So, every morning, my teacher would start me out on them, of course."

The crowd bursts out laughing. She's got a remarkable sense of timing.

"Life is funny, you know," she says, "Lots of times, it's the hard things that give us the most satisfaction. I worked hard to learn English. Today, I'm glad I did. Because I can sing everywhere in the world, and get real close to you. I can sing for you here, tonight, in Perth. It's such a lovely town, so clean, and green, so close to nature."

In her interviews, she speaks much more freely about life's everyday details than she does about her career or her plans for the future. Onstage, she presents herself as a married woman, a housewife. A star who tells the girls and women who've turned out to cheer her that the life she leads is not all that different from theirs. That her desires and needs are the same. Turning to the girls and women in the audience, she says,"I just love shopping, don't you? I bet you think I'm crazy for wanting to sleep in my own bed! do the cooking! clean house and put things away! But that's what I like."

Céline Dion is a born charmer, a master in the art of friendly persuasion, a champion at making people feel she's on their side.

"There's a rule, you know. It's not only my show." She points to the musicians and the back-up singers. "It's not only our show, here on the stage." With a broad sweep of the hand she embraces the whole stadium, from the far grandstands to the front-row seats. "Tonight, it's everybody's show." If you want to sing and dance, she tells them, go right

Céline sings without thinking when she's on tour, without reminding herself to hit one note harder than another. Her voice has a memory of its own.

ahead. And she reminds them one last time that she's just an ordinary girl. "I know what it's like to sit on a hard-backed chair for an hour and a half and listen to someone else sing." She pretends to be bored, yawns, glances at her watch, lets out a sigh. The crowd laughs. Everyone can see her face up close on the giant screens.

"Before you end up looking like that," she says, "get up, dance, sing along with us."

Céline, one of the most prominent stars of the '90s, backs up her words with actions. She doesn't merely tell her fans she's one of them, she also does all she can to help them. Unlike many other of today's superstars, she has chosen to fight not against power but against evil itself, against incurable disease, and most of all, illnesses that attack children.

Over the last few years she's become deeply involved, alongside Muhammad

Opposite page: *Céline's voice sings of love and peace, thrilling her audience everywhere she goes.*

Ali, the Brazilian soccer star Pelé, and former U.S. president Jimmy Carter, in the peaceful struggle to protect the world's children. She knows they can hear her voice, wherever they may be. And her voice sings of love and peace. She lets them know people are thinking of them, trying to help them, to bring them food, happiness, hope.

"Plenty of things make me happy," Céline says. "But not good reviews or the cheers of the crowd. What I really love is when people come up to me and tell me that one of my songs has helped them face life, to kiss and make up, to feel good about themselves or even, like 'Vole,' to accept the inevitable. That's why I sing. Singing for me is reaching out to people."

She's added a few hesitations into her monologues, a few asides that seem to wander off into nowhere. They help mask the near-mathematical efficiency of her execution and create the illusion of spontaneity. The people of Perth are convinced she's improvising, that she's telling the story for the first time, that

she's taking them into her confidence. But aside from a couple of details, everything is planned and perfectly arranged.

Perth, at the ends of the earth, isn't the only place where Céline plays on her difference. Even in France, in all her presentations and interviews, she's careful to remind people that she comes from somewhere else.

It's a funny world. The sharpest criticism of her Paris shows comes from either Quebec or from French-Canadian journalists based in Paris. These journalists know how touchy the French are about accents, and they're worried (with good reason) that Céline's will get her in hot water. The French, even in the media, are still surprised by the slightest foreign accent. But here, Céline has broken new ground. At the Olympia, the Zénith, at Bercy, in every big French hall she's performed in, she has spoken effortlessly, directly, simply. And she has touched people. That's her power. She connects. In press conferences, she is interviewed in both French and English. When a journalist uses English, she laughs and says, "Oh good, I get to practice my English." Even if her sentences are a bit off, Céline communicates with people.

She ends her monologue by saying how happy she is to sing in English today, but that doesn't mean she's forgotten her roots.

And she sings "Pour que tu m'aimes encore." In French, in Perth, on the other side of the world.

PERSONAL ASIDES

THESE MONOLOGUES OF MINE JUST GREW, NOTHING WAS EVER PLANNED. I NEVER FELT LIKE I HAD TO TALK ABOUT ONE THING OR ANOTHER. IT JUST CAME, SPONTANEOUSLY. IN FACT, I DID THEM ALONG WITH THE AUDIENCE. I NOTICED THAT WHENEVER I MENTIONED SHOPPING THE GIRLS LAUGHED OR SHOUTED. OR WHEN I SAID I LIKED STRAIGHTENING UP MY DRAWERS AND MY CLOTHES CLOSETS. IT DIDN'T TAKE ME LONG TO FIGURE OUT THAT PEOPLE LIKE IT WHEN I TALK ABOUT THE LITTLE THINGS IN LIFE. I TELL PEOPLE ABOUT WHAT I DO IN MY LIFE. THEY LIKE TO HEAR ABOUT IT, AND I LIKE TO TALK ABOUT IT. . . . I THINK THAT'S MUCH MORE INTERESTING THAN A STAR'S LIFE. AND I THINK THAT'S WHAT PEOPLE LIKE.

The Duet

FOR CÉLINE DION, HOLLYWOOD IS THE CAPITAL OF SHOW BUSINESS. A PLACE OF ALMOST MYTHICAL DIMENSIONS. THIS IS WHERE THE PEOPLE WHO HAVE CREATED THE MOST EXTRAORDINARY LEGENDS IN THE HISTORY OF THE WORLD LIVE.

YOU'D THINK THAT PEOPLE IN HOLLYWOOD HAVE SEEN IT ALL. THAT THEY'RE BLASÉ AND HARD TO PLEASE. WELL, IT'S JUST NOT SO. THE PEOPLE CROWDED INTO THE UNIVERSAL AMPHITHEATER ARE HAPPY AND CAREFREE, AND THEY LEAP TO THEIR FEET WHEN TERRY BRADFORD STEPS ONSTAGE, MIKE IN HAND, TO SING "BEAUTY AND THE BEAST" WITH CÉLINE.

TERRY BRADFORD WAS A BACK-UP SINGER IN LOS ANGELES WHEN A FRIEND INFORMED HIM CÉLINE DION WAS LOOKING FOR A SINGER WHO COULD PERFORM "BEAUTY AND THE BEAST" WITH HER—THE SAME TUNE SHE'D RECORDED WITH PEABO BRYSON. HE TURNED UP FOR THE AUDITION WITH A TOUCH OF NERVES. NORMAL ENOUGH, EVEN IF YOU'VE HAD PLENTY OF STAGE AND STUDIO EXPERIENCE, EVEN THOUGH TERRY SINGS ALL THE TIME, EVERYWHERE, IN ELEVATORS, IN PARKING GARAGES, ON THE STREET.

WHEN HIS TURN CAME HE STEPPED FORWARD, ALL ALONE ON THE STAGE, AND BEGAN TO SING. A FULL SPOTLIGHT WAS TRAINED ON HIM. HIS NERVOUSNESS EVAPORATED AFTER A COUPLE OF MEASURES, AND HE BEGAN TO SING WITH REAL PLEASURE, FORGETTING EVERYTHING, LETTING HIS VOICE SOAR, UNTIL SUDDENLY HE SAW A WOMAN EMERGE FROM THE SHADOWS AND WALK TOWARD HIM. IT WAS CÉLINE DION, AND SHE WAS SINGING THE DUET WITH HIM.

TERRY HAD NEVER SEEN ANYTHING LIKE IT. IN EVERY AUDITION HE'D EVER BEEN TO, THE HOPEFUL WAS ALONE ONSTAGE. EVERYONE DID HIS OR HER NUMBER, THANKED THE DARKNESS, AND LEFT, AND MOST OF THE TIME NOBODY SAID A WORD. THEN THEY'D GO HOME AND WAIT FOR THE PHONE TO RING. THOSE WERE THE RULES OF THE GAME.

BUT HERE WAS CÉLINE DION HERSELF, WALKING RIGHT UP TO HIM, AND SINGING A DUET WITH HIM. HE WAS SO ASTONISHED THAT HE FORGOT THE WORDS;

Right: *Céline's ability to connect with her audience is the element that puts her concerts over the top. This special quality has enabled her to gain fans worldwide.* Opposite page: *Céline's voice was heard by audiences around the globe during the "Falling into You" tour.*

THE MAGIC OF HOLLYWOOD

"SINGING IN LOS ANGELES IS QUITE AN EXPERIENCE. FOR ME, IT'S GOT A KIND OF ECHO, A KIND OF AMPLIFICATION YOU DON'T FIND IN ANY OTHER CITY. THERE'S LIKELY TO BE SOMEONE IN THE AUDIENCE LISTENING TO YOU, WATCHING YOU, AND WHO'LL COME UP TO YOU WITH A PROPOSAL THAT WILL CHANGE YOUR LIFE. A FILM, OR A SONG. IN HOLLYWOOD, ON THE *TONIGHT SHOW*, I FIRST MADE IT IN THE WORLD OF INTERNATIONAL SHOW BUSINESS. IN HOLLYWOOD, I SANG AT THE OSCARS TWO YEARS LATER. IN HOLLYWOOD, THE ARTIST FORMERLY KNOWN AS PRINCE HEARD ME SING, AND HAD THE URGE TO WRITE A SONG FOR ME, "WITH THIS TEAR." IN LOS ANGELES, AN ARTIST HAS MORE VISIBILITY THAN ANYWHERE ELSE."

she had to whisper the refrain to remind him. But she knew—both of them knew that from that moment on—they would be working together. Their voices blended together in a glorious mix that everybody loved.

Céline was delighted. And Terry was bowled over by Céline's skill, her technique, her breathing. Since that moment, they've sung together on every continent.

Encore

AS SHE TOOK THE STAGE at the Great Woods Performing Arts Center, Céline felt nervous and tense. Only four weeks earlier, in Atlanta, she had sung before the largest audience in history. Four billion people, so the media claimed. It had been a great moment, but she felt dizzy and lightheaded, like a prizefighter the day after a hard-fought victory. Still, Atlanta was only an appetizer to what was yet to come. More fame, greater popularity, still more fans.

It had been a month since she'd seen the supercharged crowds of the amphitheaters. The last concert had taken place on June 23, in Toronto. That was where she wound up the Canadian leg of the "Falling into You" tour; five weeks in eight of the ten provinces.

Tonight the tour was starting up again; 30 American cities in six weeks. Then on to Europe in mid-September. There would be no let-up until Christmas. The first shows of any tour are always the trickiest. It takes a while get rid of the kinks in the music. And it's always back to square one with the crowd. You have to reestablish your connections with the people, and you have to rediscover your confidence.

No sooner did Céline appear on the stage than the fans erupted in a touching, rousing ovation. Because they were happy to see her. And also because of her performance in Atlanta at the Olympic Games.

She gave a good show, in spite of feeling a bit down for the past few days. Before she left the stage, she shouted out, "Good night, Boston! Sweet dreams! See you again soon!"

The audience was on its feet, buoyed by its own clamor. The stage had become a black sky illuminated by tiny flickering lights, a vacuum sucking in everyone's gaze. Suddenly there came a crackling sound. And the blinding, opalescent glare of a dozen television screens lit up the stage for a brief instant. In the darkness, Céline's voice rang out, sweet and

The stage positively shines with talent as (left to right) divas Gloria Estefan, Mariah Carey, Aretha Franklin, Céline, and Shania Twain entertain the crowd at the VH-1 "Divas Live" concert in New York.

throaty. Finally she appeared—high, high up, next to Paul Picard's percussion kit.

She left the stage and darted into a kind of tent at the foot of the steps, stage right. Loulou was waiting for her with a change of costume. She helped Céline slip off her leather trousers. Manon wiped the sweat from her back and shoulders and quickly fixed her hair. Céline pulled on a body-stocking and a long dress. She emerged from the tent, with Eric standing guard. Claude Plante, waiting for her at the foot of the steps, handed her the mike and guided her along the narrow catwalk behind Frulla's keyboards and Messier's drums. For her encore, Céline would sit in the shadows, at the top of the risers that form the set. When she sang the first notes, the crowd fell silent. It was "Be-

cause You Loved Me," the theme song from the film *Up Close and Personal* starring Michelle Pfeiffer and Robert Redford. Scenes from the film played on the big screens as Céline crooned the lyrics.

❝*For all those times you stood by me*
For all the truth that you
made me see...❞

"Sing for Robert Redford?" Céline said to René when the song was first recorded. "*Any* time."

A few days after the recording session, the actor-director-producer called in person to thank Céline and congratulate her. He loved her interpretation of Diane Warren's song. The public loved it, too. It's pure velvet, soft as satin.

She repeated the last line, this time singing for the audience. "I'm everything I am because you love me." A voice cried out, "I love you, Céline." She heard it, and answered back, "I love you, too." Then she laughed and began again, from the top.

Again came a torrent of applause, cries, laughter, shouts of "I love you." She was delighted, overjoyed. In a flash, she asked the audience to sing along with her.

"I just had an idea. You sing the last line of the song along with me."

She asked Lapin to light up the crowd. He flooded the hall with white light, shattering the intimacy of the stage lighting, the music, the scenes from the film. Intimidated, the crowd sang "I'm everything I am..." in a faint voice. Céline pretended to be upset. The crowd laughed. "It's scarier for me to sing all by myself in front of you than for you to sing in front of me." And the crowd picked up the tune again, much louder this time, Céline's voice mingled with theirs. "I'm everything I am..." The music stopped to let her savor the pleasure. She sighed, "Because you loved me...."

Céline applauded. The fans did, too.

The script is simple. The trick is to carry it off every night with a partner who doesn't know what's coming. You've got to get a feel for the crowd, you've got to know that on the closing notes of "I'm everything I am...," in the tiniest fraction of a second of silence, there will be shouts and applause. Someone may cry out from the back of the

hall, "Céline, I love you," and she'll call back, "I love you, too!" She grasps hold of that moment, motions to the musicians to stop. She stretches out the silence for a second or two, then turns to the crowd and says, "I've got an idea. What if we sing that last line together?" She lets the fans know that their love makes her happy. And vice-versa.

It was quite a powerful invention, that summer's night in Boston.

Céline sang "The Power of the Dream" at the opening ceremonies of the Olympic Games in Atlanta in 1996, in front of an audience of 85,000 people, with an estimated four billion more—half the world's population!—watching on television.

The Gift

I T WAS ALMOST DARK WHEN THE LEAR JET FROM AMSTERDAM TOUCHED DOWN ON THE RAIN-SLICK RUNWAY OF THE HAMBURG AIRPORT. CÉLINE WAS HAPPY. THE TOUR WAS RUNNING ON CRUISE CONTROL. EVERYBODY WAS IN TOP FORM, PHYSICALLY AND MENTALLY. THEY WERE TOGETHER, A "BAND ON THE RUN" POWERING THEIR WAY ACROSS EUROPE. A BOISTEROUS, GOOD-HEARTED, GOOD-HUMORED BEAST OVERFLOWING WITH ENERGY AND JOY.

IN THE LAST MONTH, SINCE BERCY, THEY'D GIVEN 18 SHOWS. IN BETWEEN GRENOBLE AND NÎMES THEY'D MADE AN APPEARANCE ON *TARATATA*, FRANCE'S MOST PRESTIGIOUS TELEVISION VARIETY SHOW. CÉLINE HAD KEPT SILENT FOR TEN DAYS. EVERYTHING WAS PERFECT, OR SO IT SEEMED. THOSE LONG, UNBROKEN, DEEP SILENCES. AND THE SHOWS: EXPLOSIVE, WILD, MARVELOUSLY EXHAUSTING.

FOR MONTHS, INVITATIONS HAD BEEN FLOWING IN FROM AROUND THE WORLD. CÉLINE DION IS ONE OF A SELECT HANDFUL OF ARTISTS WHO CAN STEP BEYOND THE EVERYDAY BOUNDARIES OF SHOW BUSINESS, LEAVE THE ESTABLISHED COMMERCIAL CIRCUITS BEHIND, AND OPEN UP NEW, UNEXPLORED TERRITORIES. INVITATIONS WERE FLOODING IN FROM EVERY CORNER OF THE GLOBE. FROM THE FORMER U.S.S.R., FROM ISRAEL, FROM SOUTH AFRICA, FROM COUNTRIES SHE HAD NEVER EVEN HEARD OF.

WHAT CAN YOU SEE WHEN YOU'RE AT THE TOP? THE UNKNOWN, AS FAR AS YOU CAN SEE.

BY NOW THEY'D COME TO KNOW THE CITIES WHERE THEY WERE APPEARING. THEY ENCOUNTERED FAMILIAR FACES, THE SAME DRIVERS, THE SAME DIGNITARIES.

HAMBURG IS ALL BUSINESS, BUT IT STILL MANAGES TO BE ATTRACTIVE. DESPITE THE SEASON, THE TREES ARE STILL GREEN. CÉLINE WAS HAPPY TO BE BACK AT THE SAME HOTEL WHERE SHE HAD STAYED THE YEAR BEFORE. WHEN SHE STEPPED INTO THE ROOM, THE VERY SAME ROOM WITH ITS VIEW OVERLOOKING THE PARK, WITH ITS HEAVY DRAPES AND HUNTING SCENES ON THE WALLS, SHE THOUGHT BACK TO ALL SHE'D DONE IN LESS THAN ONE YEAR. SHE'D BEEN JUST A LITTLE GIRL BACK THEN, SHE THOUGHT. AND NOW SHE WAS A MATURE, RESPONSIBLE WOMAN.

Below: *René never tells her where he'll be, but Céline knows he's somewhere out there in the darkness, somewhere deep in the great hall where her eyes can't see, watching her every minute of the two hours her show will take. When she sings a love song, she sings it for him, every time.*
Opposite page: *French actor Gerard Depardieu told Céline, "You sing with your soul.... Your soul is visible, your whole soul, and that's your beauty."*

She had ideas, people listened to her. Her relationship with René had changed. He used to be her brain, the one who made all the decisions. Then, slowly, he began to ask for her opinion. On everything, from strategies to marketing. He was still the one with the fresh, new ideas. Ideas that stimulated and excited her, ideas that made her love her show, and her husband, and her life. Like the idea he came up with four days earlier.

When he called Céline in Amsterdam, he talked to her about the Beatles—their early days, their first gigs in Liverpool, their hard times in London, and their bohemian existence in Hamburg.

"It all started in Hamburg," René said. "When you do your show in Hamburg on the 21st, you ought to do an old Beatles song. Talk it over with Mégo. Something like 'Twist and Shout.' You could do it to wrap up the show. It would be like a gift to the people of Hamburg."

Mégo quickly located the music and arranged the orchestrations. Two days before, at the Ahoy Sports Palace, in Rotterdam, they rehearsed "Twist and Shout." Their version was fast and brief. It was a gesture that was sure to set the Hamburg Sports Hall crowd on its ear, just like it was planned to do.

There was only one thing on their minds now. Get to the end of the show as fast as possible. After the first encore, they would send their personalized version of "Twist and Shout" winging out into the crowd. That would get them on their feet. If it worked out, they could do the Beatles number after every encore. Just like they had done on the last tour, with "Everybody Dance Now." It's always a good idea to leave the crowd excited, hungry for more. Words to live by, as far as Céline is concerned.

On the Run

MORE THAN A FEW SHOWS ON THE TOUR END WITH WHAT'S CALLED A "RUNNER" IN THE TRADE. IT HAPPENS WHEN CÉLINE AND HER ENTOURAGE HAVE TO BEAT A HASTY EXIT FROM THE AMPHITHEATER. WITH THE FINAL CHORDS OF "BECAUSE YOU LOVED ME" RINGING IN THE AIR, WHILE THE STADIUM IS STILL RINGING WITH APPLAUSE, EVERYONE SPRINGS INTO MOTION. GILLES HACALA HAS ALREADY TOLD EVERYONE WHICH LIMOUSINE THEY WILL BE GETTING INTO. CÉLINE COMES DASHING OFF THE STAGE, PULLING OUT HER EARPHONES WHILE TELLING THE BAND MEMBERS AND CREW, "I LOVE YOU ALL, THANKS!" SOMEONE THROWS A COAT OVER HER SHOULDERS, AND EVERYBODY STREAKS FOR THE CARS THAT WILL SPEED OFF INTO THE NIGHT TO THE HOTEL OR TO THE AIRPORT. SOMETIMES THEY'LL EVEN HAVE A POLICE ESCORT, THEIR YELLOW AND BLUE FLASHERS LIKE STRANGE FLOWERS IN THE NIGHT, TO GUIDE THEM THROUGH THE CITY THAT'S JUST GIVEN CÉLINE AN OVATION. THEY'RE LIKE A RIVER, UNSTOPPABLE. THEN THEY'RE AIRBORNE, WHERE A PLUMP MOON AND TWINKLING STARS AWAIT THEM. THEY'RE ALL ALONE IN THE WORLD, STREAKING ACROSS THE SKY IN THEIR DELUXE JET. RENÉ, CÉLINE, AND BARRY, DAVE, ERIC, GILLES, MANON, GEORGES-HÉBERT GERMAIN, AND SUZANNE—THE PEOPLE CLOSEST TO RENÉ AND CÉLINE.

CÉLINE IS OFTEN HYPER AFTER A SHOW. SHE HUMS AND SINGS IN A SOFT VOICE THAT FLITS AND DARTS AROUND HER AS THE LIMOUSINE SPEEDS THROUGH THE STREETS, CONTINUING HER MUSIC EVEN AS THE PLANE SOARS THROUGH THE AIR, EN ROUTE TO THE NEXT DESTINATION.

THE EXIT FROM THE OLYMPIC GYMNASIUM IN SEOUL WILL GO DOWN IN THE HISTORY OF THE TOUR AS THE TIGHTEST, MOST EXCITING, AND MOST STRESSFUL OF ALL THE RUNNERS OF THE "FALLING INTO YOU" TOUR. AIR TRAFFIC CONTROL HAD INFORMED THE GROUP THAT CÉLINE'S DC–8 WOULD BE PERMITTED TO TAKE OFF FROM THE SEOUL AIRPORT ONLY BEFORE 11:30 P.M THAT NIGHT. THE AIRPORT WAS A FULL HOUR'S DRIVE AWAY FROM THE CONCERT HALL. THE CITY WAS INFAMOUS FOR ITS HUGE TRAFFIC JAMS, AND THERE WAS ALWAYS THE RISK OF GETTING STUCK,

As part of Céline's hectic lifestyle, she travels back and forth arcoss the globe numerous times a year. Here, she makes her way through London's Heathrow Airport, looking every bit the confident star.

even at such a late hour. It was necessary for the show to end no later than 10:00 in order for them to make their flight. Céline was made well aware of this before the show began.

For starters, in order to make things work, the show had to get underway on time. But at 8:00, Patrick, Eric, and Michel were still arguing with groups of young cameramen who'd plunked themselves down at various places in the hall to film the show. It took a long time and some serious discussion to convince the camermen that this just wasn't done. The show started a little late and with a bit of confusion. In order to make up some of the time they had already lost, Dave told Céline to cut the presentations short.

But the show was electrifying. There was contact with the good-natured, young crowd from the very first songs. Céline was as surprised as she was delighted. To Dave's dismay, she didn't want to leave the stage, doing one encore after another, talking with the audi-

Three of the people closest to Céline (pictured from left to right), her agent Barry Garber, René, and the author of this book, Georges-Hébert Germain, take a moment to mug for the camera en route to a stop on the tour.

ence, laughing, and enjoying the sheer pleasure of the rapport she had established with the crowd.

66 Sure, I knew I shouldn't have. Sure, I was thinking that we'd be late. But I couldn't interrupt what was going on with the crowd. 99

When Céline finally exited the stage for good, everyone sprang into action, moving as quickly as they had ever moved. They made it to the Seoul airport and managed to board the DC–8 just in the nick of time. Everyone sank into their seats, relieved. As the plane was taking off, Céline, keeping to herself, murmured her little prayer. Then she said, loudly enough for everyone to hear, "Now there's a show I'm really sorry my love missed." But she knew René would have been there if he could have.

Above: *Céline arrives at the Shrine Auditorium for the 69th Annual Academy Awards ceremony. By singing two nominated songs during the live broadcast—"Because You Loved Me" and "I Finally Found Someone"—she became the first artist ever to sing twice during an Oscars Awards ceremony.* Left: *Italian tenor Luciano Pavarotti and Céline perform together in June 1998 during the Pavarotti & Friends International '98 benefit in Modena. The benefit raised funds for the construction of a children's village in Liberia.*

The Finale

ZURICH IS SOMETHING ELSE," CÉLINE AND HER MUSICIANS ARE TELLING THE MEMBERS OF HER ENTOURAGE WHO WEREN'T WITH HER ON THE TOUR BACK IN NOVEMBER 1996. "WAIT AND SEE."

ZURICH IS THE LAST STOP ON A TOUR THAT'S ALREADY LASTED NEARLY THREE YEARS. OR REALLY, A SUCCESSION OF TOURS, ONE AFTER THE OTHER.

THE LAST SHOWS ON A TOUR ARE ALWAYS SPECIAL. "BUT ZURICH IS DIFFERENT," CÉLINE SAID. "YOU'VE NEVER SEEN A CROWD ANYWHERE ELSE DO WHAT THEY DO." AND LEFT IT AT THAT. AFTER ALL, ONE NEVER KNOWS. MAYBE LAST NOVEMBER'S EXALTATION WON'T HAPPEN AGAIN.

IT DOES, HOWEVER. MORE THAN ONCE. MORE POWERFULLY THAN ANYONE COULD HAVE BELIEVED. AND SOONER THAN ANYONE EXPECTED. ON THE LAST CHORDS OF "RIVER DEEP, MOUNTAIN HIGH," THE MIGHTY MASS OF MUSIC SEEMS TO EXPLODE INTO A MILLION TINY FRAGMENTS JUST AS THE LIGHTS GO OUT. THERE'S AN INSTANT OF DARKNESS IN THE CONCERT HALL, AND A FRACTION OF A SECOND OF SILENCE. THEN COMES THE APPLAUSE.

EVERY NIGHT, EVERYWHERE, THE SAME THING HAPPENS. IT NEVER FAILS. IN THE MIDDLE OF THE TUMULT THAT FOLLOWS THE EXPLOSIVE FINALE OF "RIVER DEEP, MOUNTAIN HIGH" YOU CAN HEAR A TINY, SILVERY LAUGH. THE FAINTEST TINKLE. YOU PROBABLY WOULD HAVE TO KNOW ABOUT IT TO HEAR IT. IT'S THE LAUGH OF A HAPPY LITTLE GIRL. CÉLINE MAY NOT EVEN REALIZE IT, BUT EVERY TIME PEOPLE GET TO THEIR FEET TO APPLAUD HER, SHE EMITS THAT TINY PEAL OF LAUGHTER.

AT THE LEITZEGRUND STADIUM IN ZURICH ON THE LAST NIGHT OF THE TOUR IT WAS DIFFERENT. WHEN THE LIGHTS CAME BACK ON, THE TRIUMPH WAS ALREADY SECURE. PEOPLE WERE WAVING THEIR OUTSTRETCHED HANDS AT CÉLINE. ALL YOU COULD SEE IN THE HUGE LEITZEGRUND STADIUM WAS THE QUIVERING OF 100,000 HANDS, FINGERS SPREAD WIDE, HIDING FACES AND FORMING A WINDSWEPT FIELD OF FLOWERS, AND FROM THAT FIELD SOUNDED A LONG, DRAWN-OUT "AHHH," SOFT

Right: *The fans in Zurich demonstrate their own distinctive version of the wave.* Below: *Céline and her band are able to create a fresh, thrilling performance every night of the tour, electrifying fans around the world with their talents.*

at first, then swelling until it filled the stadium.... That's what had made such an impression on Céline and her musicians in November 1996. But it came too late on that night, almost at the end of a show that had never really gotten off the ground. At first the crowd reacted slowly, as if it had other things on its mind, as if it were sad. Céline did everything she could and then some. Then, slowly but surely, the electricity began to build. After the last song the people had come out with that strange call and waved their arms. It was beautiful, strange, frightening. When the British stamp their feet to create an earsplitting din, when the Scandinavians shout "ohey, ohey," when the Americans start clapping in unison, when the French cry "un autre! un autre!" it's always impressive. But when the Zurichers put their mind to it, they do things no one else can. Céline had the presence of mind to ask them to do it again "because what you do is so beautiful, and so rare." Lapin

turned his spotlights on the audience. And Céline motioned to one of the cameramen onstage to record the incredible crowdscape.

This time, the Zurichers didn't wait for an encore. As soon as Céline caught the mood, she had them start the wave with their own particular twist. The audience was on its feet in two or three seconds, arms waving back and forth, like light shimmering on a slow-rolling sea.

It was a fantastic, unforgettable show—one of the most beautiful and most moving of the entire tour. It was the perfect end to the tour. Many of Céline's friends and collaborators had followed the final days of the "Falling into You" tour, in whole or in part. There was Marc Verreault, Ben Kaye, and Lloyd Brault who, in spite of the rain that kept on falling all over Europe, managed to get in a round of golf every afternoon. At night, along with Barry, Dave, René, Vito, and René's daughter, Anne-Marie, they would take in the show from the control booth right in the middle of the main floor. Patrick Angélil came to get them during the encore, and they would flow through the noisy crowd like a little river, flashing their passes and making their way backstage.

In Zurich, as Céline sang "Because You Loved Me" as an encore, René led Anne-Marie, Marc Verreault, and Suzanne Gingue onto the stage. Standing there in the darkness, they saw the breathtaking sight of the crowd head-on.

Those tens of thousands of faces and upraised arms. They saw Céline from behind, running back and forth across the stage like a surfer hurrying to catch the next wave. Then the musicians and back-up singers joined her, waving to the audience. Afterward, all around the stage, backstage, and in the dressing rooms, for a good part of the night, people talked, kissed, and cried. It was the finale. The next day, the whole crew would leave for Montreal. In Céline Dion's life, it was a historic moment.

Barbra Streisand has always been one of Céline's idols. The two became friends after Céline sang "I Finally Found Someone" as a last-minute replacement for Barbra at the 1997 Academy Awards ceremony. Here they are together onstage at a David Foster tribute.

Her Heart Goes On

IN EARLY SPRING 1997, René learned that composer James Horner was hoping Céline would sing his love theme for James Cameron's *Titanic*. He knew that Céline was perfect for the project. René and Céline went into their studio and worked hard to prepare a demo tape for Cameron.

Knowing that, like the ocean liner, this movie was meant to be unequaled, Céline sought deep inside herself for her sweetest, warmest voice, the one she knew to be the most touching. Horner and Cameron were instantly seduced. Cameron believed she had captured "the spirit of the movie," and Horner said the demo was brilliant. Céline didn't have to rework it in a studio. The song—straight from her demo—was heard around the globe just as she had recorded it. Within months, the movie's soundtrack, buoyed by her Number One single "My Heart Will Go On," sold 25 million copies worldwide.

The previous summer, Céline developed a passion for golf that literally changed her life and strengthened the bond she had with René. After the "Falling into You" tour, René had convinced her to take some classes. Very quickly, she developed a love of early mornings, fresh air, and the smell of freshly cut grass covered with dew. She discovered that golf is more than a sport or a game. It is a way of life, a strict discipline demanding determination and rigor and supplying intense moments of joy. She learned more about herself, just as she had with singing and her music. Céline and René spent that summer of

In the summer of 1997, Céline discovered a new passion—golf. It is one she can share with René, and it allows the two of them to enjoy precious time alone together. A "night person" on tour, at home she rises early to hit the golf course with René.

1997 playing golf. Often alone, and perfectly happy.

On March 30, 1998, Céline's 30th birthday, Patrick Angélil threw a huge surprise party. Céline was truly happy; her happiness was genuine and radiant. Céline was happy with what she had already accomplished, but she was happier still about her future. It seemed more exciting and intriguing than ever.

❝I am as much in love with René as on the first day. It is the same with my music and my life. And at the same time, it seems more than ever, that everything around me is new. My house, my songs, my show, my passions, my loves. This is probably where I have been the luckiest and what I consider my greatest achievement—I have this constantly renewed life, always starting afresh, and passions, friendships, loves that last.❞

In August, Céline teamed once more with her musicians to prepare for the "Let's Talk About Love" world tour, which opened to rave reviews on August 21, 1998, in Boston. It is slated to run into the new millennium. A gigantic show, prepared with great care and time, with energy and money; every aspect is state of the art. "The most important of my life" according to Céline, the one she had always dreamed of, the show of a 30-year-old woman, free, autonomous, in love....

Above: *After performing the Oscar-winning song "My Heart Will Go On" (Best Original Song) from the film* Titanic *at the Academy Awards ceremony on March 23, 1998, Céline shows off her necklace, fashioned after the one seen in the movie and sold at a charity auction for more than two million dollars.* Left: *At the premiere of* Titanic *in December 1997, the diva looked positively elegant in pearls. Could she possibly have foreseen the gigantic success of the movie and the album featuring her song?*

CÉLINE DION DISCOGRAPHY

LA VOIX DU BON DIEU (1981)
CELINE DION CHANTE NOËL (1981)
TELLEMENT J'AI D'AMOUR (1982)
LES CHEMINS DE MA MAISON (1983)
MÉLANIE (1984)
LES PLUS GRANDS SUCCÉS (1984)
C'EST POUR TOI (1985)
CELINE DION EN CONCERT (1985)
LES CHANSONS EN OR (1986)
INCOGNITO (1987)
UNISON (1990)
DION CHANTE PLAMONDON (1991)
CELINE DION (1992)
THE COLOUR OF MY LOVE (1993)
CELINE DION À L'OLYMPIA (1994)
D'EUX/THE FRENCH ALBUM (1995)
FALLING INTO YOU (1996)
LIVE À PARIS (1996)
LET'S TALK ABOUT LOVE (1997)
S'IL SUFFISAIT D'AIMER (1998)
THESE ARE SPECIAL TIMES (1998)